CULTURES OF THE WORLD®

IRAQ

Susan M. Hassig/Laith Muhmood Al Adely

BENCHMARK BOOKS

MARSHALL CAVENDISH
NEW YORK

PICTURE CREDITS
Cover photo: © Jonathan Wright/Bruce Coleman, Inc.
AFP: 10, 24, 54, 59, 67, 74, 84, 110, 113, 118 • Art Directors & TRIP: 16, 88, 96, 124 • Camera Press: 44 • Christine Osborne Pictures: 3, 4, 14, 18, 19, 22, 36, 39, 40, 41, 52, 56, 57, 61, 63, 66, 68, 69, 71, 73, 75, 76, 77, 78, 79, 87, 90, 91, 94, 95, 97, 101, 107, 112, 120, 121, 128 • Getty Images/Hulton Archive: 20, 25, 28, 30, 32, 49 • Hajah Halijah: 80, 83, 114 • The Image Bank: 12, 15, 21, 35, 55, 98, 99, 100, 119, 122 • Klingwalls Geografiska Färgfotos: 6, 34, 42, 45, 48, 65, 85, 92, 93, 102, 126 • Lonely Planet Images: 1, 50, 62, 131 • HBL Network: 5 • Reuters/Bettmann: 23 • Reuters NewMedia Inc./CORBIS: 26 • Jamie Simson: 9, 11, 13, 17, 38, 51, 53, 58, 60, 70, 103, 109, 115 • Times Media: 123 • Topham Picturepoint: 47 • Nik Wheeler: 8, 64, 72, 108 • World Religions Photo Library: 130

CO-AUTHOR'S ACKNOWLEDGMENT AND DEDICATION
I would like to credit the original author, Ms. Susan M. Hassig, for laying a very firm foundation with her factual contribution, which will give readers a deeper understanding and perspective of Iraq and its remarkable but long-tormented citizens, and their customs, religions, artistic interests, language, and general lifestyle. This revised edition is dedicated to all the suffering people of Iraq.
—Laith Muhmood Al Adely, March 31, 2003

PUBLISHER'S ACKNOWLEDGMENT
With thanks to Marylee Knowlton for her expert help with this and all titles in the Cultures of the World series.

PRECEDING PAGE
An Iraqi family enjoys a picnic on a blanket in the city of Samarra in Salah ad Din province.

Marshall Cavendish Corporation
99 White Plains Road
Tarrytown, NY 10591
Website: www.marshallcavendish.com

© 1993, 2004 by Times Media Private Limited
All rights reserved. First edition 1993. Second edition 2004.

Originated and designed by
Times Books International, an imprint of
Times Media Private Limited, a member of
Times International Publishing

Printed in Malaysia

Library of Congress Cataloging-in-Publication Data
Hassig, Susan M., 1969-
Iraq / by Susan M. Hassig, Laith Muhmood Al Adely.— 2nd ed.
    p. cm. — (Cultures of the world)
Summary: Explores the geography, history, government, economy, people, and culture of Iraq.
    ISBN 0-7614-1668-4
Includes bibliographical references and index.
1. Iraq—Juvenile literature. [1. Iraq.] I. Al Adely, Laith Muhmood. II. Title. III. Series.
DS70.62.H374 2003
956.7—dc21   2003010082

7 6 5 4 3

CONTENTS

Fan-shaped date palms stretch as far as the eye can see along the Shatt al-Arab, where the Tigris and Euphrates converge.

3

Baghdad became Iraq's capital city in the eighth century A.D.

INTRODUCTION

IRAQ IS A POLITICALLY VOLATILE COUNTRY that dominated news headlines around the world many times in the last decade of the 20th century and the early years of the 21st century. While Iraqi politics has triggered strong negative reactions from the international community, its ancient history has fascinated and awed.

With a history going back more than 6,000 years, Iraq was the site of the world's earliest civilization—Mesopotamia. The growth of Mesopotamia and Iraq followed the course of two great rivers—the Tigris and the Euphrates.

Iraq is a country of great geographic diversity, with mountains in the north, vast deserts in the south, and marshlands along the rivers. The ruggedness of Iraq's terrain is reflected in the people, who have lived through war and poverty, holding on to their customs, religious beliefs, and artistic interests. With the fall of military dictatorship in 2003, a new hope dawns for a brighter future for Iraq.

GEOGRAPHY

THE REPUBLIC OF IRAQ is located in southwestern Asia. Iraq's neighbors are Turkey to the north, Syria and Jordan to the west, Iran to the east, and Kuwait and Saudi Arabia to the south.

Iraq is almost completely surrounded by land except for a 25 mile-wide (65 km-wide) outlet at its southeastern tip, where it meets the Persian Gulf. Iraq is 865 miles (2,241 km) long from north to south, and 775 miles (2,008 km) wide at its broadest point. The country has a total land area of around 166,859 square miles (432,162 square km), slightly larger than the U.S. state of California.

The name for ancient Iraq, Mesopotamia, which means land between the rivers, describes the valleys of the Tigris and Euphrates. The two rivers begin in the mountains of eastern Turkey and flow past northern Syria before reaching the lower valleys of Iraq. The 1,180-mile (3,057-km) Tigris is fed by rivers flowing from the Zagros Mountains; the 2,235-mile (5,791-km) Euphrates has no tributaries. The well-drained Tigris-Euphrates valley has many lakes.

GEOGRAPHIC REGIONS

The land between the rivers is called the Fertile Crescent because it has supported agriculture for thousands of years. Beyond the fertile valley between the Tigris and Euphrates rivers, the topography and vegetation of Iraq changes drastically. Toward the west and south the landscape transforms into a vast, dry desert; toward the north it becomes a cold, mountainous region.

Only 15 percent of Iraqi land, in the northern foothills and mountains, rises more than 1,500 feet (457 m). Most of the country is less than 1,000 feet (305 m) above sea level. The lowest point, at sea level, occurs where the Tigris and Euphrates rivers flow into the Persian Gulf.

THE DELTA The delta makes up the southeastern part of Iraq between the capital city (Baghdad) and the Persian Gulf. The delta is mostly a wide alluvial plain. Near the city of Basra, where the marshy lake Hawr al-Hammar lies south of the Euphrates, many winding waterways form marshlands where Arabs have for a long time lived in reed houses. These marshlands, the largest in the Middle East, shrank drastically in the 1990s.

The Tigris and Euphrates converge in the delta on the Shatt al-Arab, which flows into the Persian Gulf. Basra, Iraq's only port city, lies on the banks of the Shatt al-Arab. Part of the Shatt al-Arab forms a boundary between Iran and Iraq. Most Iraqis live in this region, from the simple marsh Arabs to the sophisticates of the large cities.

Thousands of years ago, the fertile soil of the Tigris-Euphrates valley encouraged nomads to settle there and establish a civilization. The valley today remains the life source of the Iraqi people. However, the Tigris is also a threat to the capital and other cities; frequent spring floods are diverted to protect the cities and irrigate farmlands.

STEPPE-DESERT PLAINS The area west of the delta region consists of the steppe-desert plains. Most of this area is part of the arid Syrian Desert.

The vast reaches of the plains are sparsely populated because of the harsh climate and rocky terrain. A few channels from the Euphrates run through this region, but they are dry for most of the year. In the southwest, the rocky Al-Hajara Desert extends into Saudi Arabia; it is a popular stop for Bedouin nomads.

NORTHERN FOOTHILLS North of the city of Samarra and between the Tigris and Euphrates lie the northern foothills. This region of grassy plains and rolling hills receives generous rainfall. There are few trees, but the foothills produce an abundance of grain. This area has cooler summers and colder winters than the delta region. The foothills are the site of many archeological ruins, including the ancient city of Assyria.

Reed houses of Iraqis who live in the marshy region by the banks of the Euphrates.

NORTHEASTERN MOUNTAINS This region is inhabited mainly by the Kurds, a non-Arab people. The Zagros Mountains rise north of the cities of Mosul and Kirkuk and extend into Iran and Turkey. The terrain consists of mountains, valleys, terraced hills, and pastures. Located here is Iraq's highest mountain, Haji Ibrahim, which stands at 11,891 feet (3,624 m).

The Kurds live in the valleys and foothills of the Zagros Mountains where they cultivate the land. The region has some of Iraq's richest oil fields. However, being so remote, the mountains are also a haven for rebels and criminals.

CLIMATE

Iraq's climate varies dramatically. The north is hot in summer and freezing cold in winter; the east and southeast are tropical and very humid; and the west is desert and very dry. On average, nationwide summer temperatures range from 72°F (24°C) to 110°F (43°C), while temperatures in winter dip to near freezing in the north and to 60°F (16°C) in the south.

The summer season, between June and September, is the hottest time of the year, when Iraq is visited by a northwesterly wind, the *sharqi* (SHAHR-kee). The *sharqi* is a dry and dusty wind that is often accompanied by dust storms. The scorching sun produces high temperatures of up to 120°F (49°C) along the Persian Gulf. In the winter months, from December through March, the southern and southeastern parts are visited by the *shamal* (shah-MAHL), a cool and moist wind blowing from the sea.

Iraq is a dry country with relatively little rainfall. Much of the rain falls in the winter and spring months, while summers are hot and dry. The annual rainfall is about 16 inches (103 cm) in the delta region and 20 to 40 inches (129 to 258 cm) in the northern foothills and in the mountains. Rain evaporates quickly in the delta, so Iraqis depend on irrigation to cultivate the soil. Destructive floods can occur in the rare event of heavy rainfall.

FLORA

Alpine plants grow in the higher altitudes of Iraq such as the Zagros Mountains. Alpine plants can withstand the freezing winters. Hawthorn, juniper, maple, and oak trees also thrive in the mountains. However, excessive logging has led to the loss of some oak forests.

Vegetation is fairly sparse, largely because of the arid climate and the high salt content of the soil. Desert flora such as the rockrose and storksbill survive the dry summer months and bloom in spring after the rains. Iraq's desert flora is similar to the vegetation in Arizona and New Mexico. Orange and lemon trees grow in central and southern Iraq.

Dates, a dark and extremely sweet fruit, grow on palm trees in many parts of Iraq. Dates are used in a variety of dishes, especially desserts. Other parts of the date palm are also useful. For example, palm fronds are used for weaving, and date pits are ground into a beverage. Because the date palm is so useful, Iraqis refer to it as the eternal plant or the tree of life. Iraq was one of the world's largest exporters of dates in the 1970s, but since the 1980s date production in Iraq has fallen to less than a quarter of what it used to be.

Reeds grow in marshes and swamps along the Tigris and Euphrates. These plants are used by the cosmetics, medicinal drugs, and food industries. Buttercup and saltbrush grow in the plains and marshlands.

Above: **Harvesting dates.**

Opposite: **An Iraqi family crosses a flooded Baghdad street on a cart. There is no proper drainage, so floods occur when heavy rains cause the rivers to overflow.**

Camels are a common sight in the deserts of southern and western Iraq. Camels are herded by nomadic Bedouins.

FAUNA

Iraq has relatively little wildlife for its size. One of the most common animals in Iraq is the camel, which can survive on very little water while traveling great distances. The camel has been domesticated to transport heavy loads across the desert.

Iraq's vast deserts may seem to be void of life by day, but at night they come alive as a variety of nocturnal animals emerge from their shady daytime holes. Two common kinds of desert creatures are lizards and snakes. Other wild desert fauna include hyenas, jackals, and gazelles. Predators such as bears, leopards, foxes, wild boars, and wolves roam the mountainous regions of northern Iraq.

The Tigris and Euphrates contain freshwater fish that people catch for food. Birds such as ducks and geese are found near rivers or swampy marshes. Birds of prey include vultures, eagles, and buzzards. A common bird in Iraq is the stork, which often nests on the roofs of houses. House owners believe they are blessed with luck if a stork nests on their roof.

THE WORLD'S OLDEST CIVILIZATION

According to the Muslim, Christian, and Jewish faiths, the first man and woman were Adam and Eve. The Christian and Jewish faiths also believe that Adam and Eve lived in the Garden of Eden, believed to be at Al-Qurna in southern Iraq (*below, southern marshlands*).

Besides being the mythical site of the birth of humankind, Iraq is also home to the world's earliest civilization. In the mid-19th century, archeologists discovered ruined buildings, clay tablets, and pottery from the ancient Sumerian civilization dating back to 3500 B.C. Remains were discovered of the world's oldest cities—Ur, Eridu, Uruk, Lagash, and Nippur.

Historians believe that Mesopotamia was the world's first civilization to experiment with writing. Cuneiform, or wedge-shaped writing, has been found on clay tablets from ancient Sumer—evidence of the oldest written language ever discovered.

CITIES

Rapid urbanization in the last 50 years has seen more people moving to the cities. Between 1975 and 2000, Baghdad's population grew by over 70 percent. About 77 percent of Iraqis now live in the large cities or the suburbs. Many cities are located near the Tigris or Euphrates.

BAGHDAD Iraq's capital city is located on the banks of the Tigris in the delta region. Baghdad has a population of about 5.8 million.

Baghdad was a small village until A.D. 762, when it became the new capital of the Abbasid dynasty. By A.D. 800 Baghdad had become a center of culture and education. It prospered until 1258, when it was invaded and ransacked by the Mongols, a warlike people from Mongolia in eastern Asia. Baghdad declined steadily in importance until the mid-16th century, when it prospered again after it became part of the Ottoman empire. In 1920 Baghdad became the capital of Iraq under British rule.

Besides being the center of government, Baghdad is also a major industrial city, with food processing, cement, and oil industries. The city is a beautiful mix of the old and the modern. The Karkh district on the western bank of the Tigris is the modern section, filled with high-rise buildings and elegant avenues. Many hotels and foreign banks are found here. Rusafah district, on the eastern bank of the Tigris, is the old part of the city, with narrow, dusty streets and outdoor bazaars.

The capital city suffered a great deal of damage during the gulf wars. The main targets of bombing raids by coalition forces were military and government buildings, but many civilian buildings were also destroyed in the process. Reconstruction is ongoing, although this has been hampered by continued combat and international sanctions that prevented other countries from supplying Iraq with construction materials.

BASRA Iraq's chief port is 75 miles (194 km) inland from the Persian Gulf. Founded in A.D. 636, Basra is now Iraq's second largest city, with a population of 1.4 million.

In the 1960s and 1970s, Basra was a major oil-refining center and a major commercial center, exporting Iraq's oil and dates.

Basra was badly damaged during the Iraq-Iran war in the 1980s and in the gulf wars. Since 1991 the city had recovered to a certain extent, but with the latest war and UN sanctions, Basra is a far cry from its peak in the 1970s.

MOSUL Iraq's third largest city is the urban center of northern Iraq. Mosul is located on the western bank of the Tigris in the northeastern Kurdish region.

Most of Mosul's 1.1 million inhabitants are Kurdish or Arab Muslims. There is also a large Christian community. Mosul depends on oil, cotton, grain, fruit, and sheep for trade. Because of the abundance of cotton, weaving is a popular craft in Mosul. As in Basra, business in Mosul suffered during 12 years of sanctions.

KIRKUK Iraq's fourth largest city and largest Kurdish city is located in northeastern Iraq. Kirkuk is a major hub for the oil industry. Oil pipelines run from here through Syria, Lebanon, and Turkey to the Mediterranean ports. When sanctions were imposed in 1990, equipment depreciation reduced Kirkuk's oil production to half its capacity. Kirkuk's population of 650,000 is rapidly growing as more people move from the countryside to the cities.

A view of Baghdad by the banks of the Tigris. About 30 percent of Iraqis live in Baghdad.

HISTORY

THE WORLD'S FIRST known civilization is believed to have begun in Iraq around 3500 B.C. Some of the earliest evidence that archeologists have found are cylinder seals, which people pressed into soft clay to create a signature that they marked their letters with.

Mesopotamia, as ancient Iraq was called, saw the rise of the 13 city-states of Sumer in 3500 B.C. in southeastern Iraq. This highly advanced society built irrigation canals and pyramid-shaped temples called *ziggurat* (ZIG-goo-raht), and developed weapons and accurate measuring instruments. The Sumerians also developed a writing system called cuneiform.

Around 2334 B.C. King Sargon I led the Akkadians to conquer Sumer, but the Babylonians conquered Mesopotamia in 1900 B.C. and ruled until 1600 B.C. The most famous Babylonian ruler, King Hammurabi, unified the city-states and created the first known comprehensive code of law.

The last great civilization in Mesopotamia was the Assyrian empire, which lasted from the ninth to the seventh century B.C. The Assyrians were headed by a ruthless monarchy that controlled Mesopotamia and neighboring Syria. Besides their might in war, the Assyrians were known for their great monuments, as excavations at Nineveh, Ashur, Khorsabad, and other sites have shown. By the early seventh century B.C., revolts by the Chaldeans of southern Sumer had ended Assyrian rule. Nebuchadnezzar II, the most famous Chaldean king, who reigned from 605 to 562 B.C., was known not only for his military victories but also for the magnificence of his capital, Babylon.

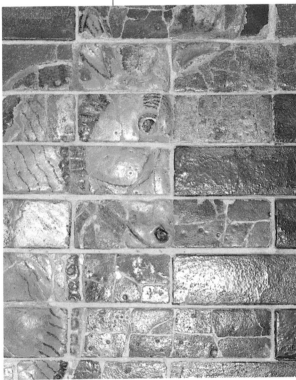

Above: **These blue-glazed tiles with the relief of a bull once belonged to the Ishtar Gate of Babylon.**

Opposite: **A minaret at the ruins of Samarra. Built in the ninth century, spiral ramps wind around the building. This minaret is believed to be part of the largest mosque ever built.**

Greek ruins in Iraq date back to the time of Alexander the Great.

FOREIGN CONQUESTS

After the Chaldeans, a new history in Mesopotamia began as foreign civilizations invaded and conquered the country.

The first invaders were the Persians, who conquered the region and added it to their empire in 550 B.C. The area remained under Persian rule until Alexander the Great conquered it in 331 B.C. The Greeks introduced metropolitan cities and scientific rationalism, and improved irrigation systems, trade, and commerce. Alexander had wonderful plans to restore the old temples of Babylon but died of malaria at the young age of 32. His successors were weak, and the Greeks lost Mesopotamia to the Persian Parthians in 126 B.C.

For about 300 years, Mesopotamia was controlled by the Parthians, migrants from Turkestan and northern Iraq. The invaders were true fighters, who overthrew Greek rule but preserved the cities and Greek culture. For brief periods, from A.D. 116 to 117 and again from A.D. 198 to 217, the Romans occupied Mesopotamia. The Parthians regained control until A.D. 224, when the Iranian Sassanids swept in from the east.

One of the most important conquests occurred in A.D. 637, when followers of Prophet Muhammad led troops into Mesopotamia and converted the people to Islam. By A.D. 650 the Sassanids had been defeated and Iraq had become the Islamic state it is today.

THE GOLDEN AGE

A great period in Iraqi and Islamic history occurred during the Abbasid caliphate from A.D. 750 to 1258, led by the descendants of Prophet Muhammad. Under the Abbasids, Iraq experienced a golden age. The capital city, Baghdad, was organized in three concentric circles: civilians lived in the outer ring, the army in the second ring, and the rulers in the center. The capital became the center of political power and culture in the Middle East, and the country became an important trading center between Asia and the Mediterranean Sea.

Baghdad reached its peak during the reign of the caliph Harun al-Rashid in the eighth century. This was the time great monuments were built, and the collection of Arab folktales called *A Thousand and One Nights* was written. In the ninth century, Arabic numerals and a decimal system were invented, irrigation systems improved, and diplomatic relations with other states established. By the 10th century, however, the caliphate's influence had declined, as the caliphs focused too much on the cities and too little on the rural areas.

In 1258 Iraq was overrun by Mongol hordes streaming down the plains of Central Asia. They destroyed Baghdad and killed the last Abbasid caliph. To this day many Iraqis believe that Iraq never truly recovered from the destruction inflicted by the Mongols. Iraq remained a neglected part of the Mongol empire until 1534, when the Turks seized it and made it a part of the Ottoman empire.

In ceremonial uniform, King Faisal II sits on a throne at the Guildhall during a 1956 state visit to London. He and his family were assassinated two years later.

BRITISH MANDATE

In 1917, during World War I, the British invaded and captured Baghdad from the Turks. By 1918 they had invaded Mosul and claimed all of Iraq, except the Kurdish region in the north.

The British conquest of Iraq aimed to limit German influence in the Middle East. The British feared that the German alliance with Turkey would disrupt oil lines between Britain, the Middle East, and India. The Arabs cooperated with the British in fighting the Turks on the promise of eventual independence.

In 1920 a British mandate was formed that created an Iraqi state. The Iraqis, realizing that they had still not reached their goal of total independence, organized a number of revolts. In 1922 Britain agreed to grant Iraq independence by 1932.

INDEPENDENCE

In October 1932, Iraq was admitted to the League of Nations as an independent monarchy. Independent Iraq faced many problems internally and with neighboring countries. King Faisal ruled Iraq until his death in 1933.

Faisal's son, Ghazi, was unable to pull the divided country together. Ghazi's rule was interrupted by a military coup, yet he stayed in control until his death in an automobile accident in 1939.

After Ghazi's death, his infant son, Faisal II, became the new ruler of Iraq. Faisal II's uncle, Amir Abd al-Ilah, acted as regent until he was old enough to rule.

KING FAISAL II

Faisal II was the king of Iraq between 1953 and 1958. During his reign, Iraq suffered from the aftermath of World War II and his own political mistakes. In the late 1940s, the economy plummeted due to worldwide shortages and a mass exodus of affluent Jews from Iraq to Israel.

On July 14, 1958, an uproar began in the streets of Baghdad as the people of Iraq revolted against the monarchy. The revolutionaries, led by General Abdul Karim Kassem, publicly executed King Faisal II, Amir Abd al-Ilah, and other members of the royal family. This revolution was one in a series of military coups that plagued Iraq until the successful retention of power by the Baath (bah-AHTH) Party in 1968.

Left: **The Martyrs' Monument is dedicated to all who died fighting for their country.**

p22: **Monument to the Baath Party, which took control of Iraq in a bloodless coup in 1968.**

MILITARY COUPS

In 1963 the Kassem regime was replaced by the Baath Party, which organized a military coup that lasted less than a year. The party's lack of definitive programs and leaders permitted the Nasserites, a group led by Abd as-Salaam Arif, who had played a leading role in the 1958 revolution, to overthrow them.

In 1966 Arif was killed in a helicopter crash. His militarily weak brother, Abd ar-Rahman Arif, became president. In 1968 a highly organized and militarily strong Baath Party dominated by Ahmad Hassan al-Bakr and Saddam Hussein overthrew President Arif and took control of Iraq.

Al-Bakr became the president of Iraq, and Hussein the vice-president and deputy secretary-general of the Baath Party. In 1979 al-Bakr resigned, and Hussein became president.

HISTORY OF THE BAATH PARTY

Two Syrian students named Salah ad-Din al-Bitar and Michel Aflaq founded the Baath Party in the early 1940s. The students developed a political party based on the ideals of freedom, socialism, unity, and a secular government. The ideals of the Baath Party became ingrained in the minds of a few Iraqis during a wave of communism in the 1950s.

By 1955 the Baath Party had grown to some 300 members. The membership of the party grew further in 1958 as many Iraqis became disgusted with the communist policies of the Iraqi leader, Kassem. The party continued to increase in strength and membership and was the only political party officially permitted in Iraq. Some of its early ideals were no longer even a memory.

THE IRAQ-IRAN WAR

In February 1979, the ayatollah of Iran, Sayyid Ruhollah Musavi Khomeini, overthrew the shah of Iran and made Iran an Islamic republic. Saddam Hussein, fearing that Iran would agitate a rebellion among the Shi'a majority in Iraq, sent his troops into Iran for a full-scale war. This was also a means for Hussein to gain full control of the Shatt al-Arab and of the oil-producing Iranian border province of Khuzestan. The war lasted eight years, incurred an estimated total economic loss of US$1.2 billion, and claimed the lives of a million Iraqis and Iranians.

The Iraq-Iran War commenced on September 22, 1980, and finally ended in August 1988. Due to the political changes in Iran at the time, Iraq had invaded a disorganized Iran. In the first few months of the bitter war, Iraqi forces laid siege to several Iranian towns and killed hundreds of troops.

The Iranians gathered strength and retaliated in the spring of 1982, forcing the Iraqis to retreat. Underestimating the new strength of the Iranian troops, Hussein attempted to settle the war. The bitter Iranians refused his peace offering and launched a massive offensive. They came very close to capturing the Iraqi port city of Basra, which the Iraqis defended at a huge cost to human life.

In 1986 the Iraqis used chemical weapons in the war, with devastating results. With increased military aid from the West, Iraq gained the upper hand. The Iranians, realizing that the tide of war was turning against them, agreed to a ceasefire in August 1988. Neither side emerged victorious. For both countries, the war was a tragedy with enormous social and economic consequences.

THE 1991 GULF WAR

In the aftermath of the Iraq-Iran war, the Iraqi economy was devastated. With depressed oil prices affecting Iraq's revenue, Hussein turned his attention to Kuwait.

Hussein and the Al Sabah family ruling the Kuwaiti emirate had a number of disagreements, such as the oil fields lying on the disputed Iraq-Kuwait border. The border had been a source of friction since 1958, when Iraq became a republic, as various regimes in Baghdad since then had laid claim to Kuwait.

Other issues such as low oil prices caused by Kuwaiti overproduction and Kuwait's insistence on recovering money that it loaned, or in Hussein's eyes donated, to Iraq in its war effort against Iran were also sources of irritation to Hussein.

Iraqi civilians and civil defence workers survey the damage near a Christian church after a bombing raid in Baghdad.

On August 2, 1990, Hussein ordered his troops to invade Kuwait. In a matter of hours, the ruling Al Sabah family fled to exile in Saudi Arabia. The worldwide reaction to the invasion was swift. The United Nations imposed economic sanctions on Iraq that rendered the country unable to export its oil and that halted imports into Iraq and froze Iraqi assets overseas. A military alliance formed predominantly by the United States and Britain that included troops from Middle Eastern nations, other European nations, and Australia started gathering in the deserts of Saudi Arabia close to the Iraq-Kuwait border.

The United Nations passed a resolution in December 1990 authorizing the use of force against Iraq unless its troops withdrew from Kuwait by January 15, 1991. The deadline passed without any Iraqi withdrawal, and the allies launched an air attack on military installations and government targets in Iraq as well as on the Iraqi garrison in Kuwait. The first 24 hours of the air attack saw greater bomb tonnage than what U.S. forces had dropped during all of World War II. Hussein had Soviet planes for air defense, which quickly proved inadequate against the high-technology fighter planes, weapons, and other war apparatus of the allied forces.

On February 24, the allies launched a ground offensive, which lasted 100 hours. They moved into Kuwait with minimum Iraqi resistance; what was left of the Iraqi forces in Kuwait retreated to Iraq or surrendered. On February 28, 1991, a ceasefire was signed at Safwan in southern Iraq.

Hussein claimed that the war was a victory for Iraq, even though 100,000 Iraqis had died and terrible damage had been done to Kuwait's oil fields and sea lanes by retreating Iraqis' acts of sabotage and allied forces' attacks.

A Patriot missile launcher sits in the desert during Operation Desert Storm. U.S. Patriot missiles were used to combat Iraqi scud missiles in the Gulf War.

GOVERNMENT

UNTIL 2003 Iraq had a system of government that was similar to that of many other countries in the Middle East. A dictatorship run by Saddam Hussein since 1979, Iraq had ministries, courts, and departments to run the activities of a government.

Forces loyal to Saddam Hussein maintained order by relying heavily on repression in the forms of imprisonment, torture, and murder. Of the 23 ministries, the largest government agency was the Ministry of the Interior, which consisted of the police and the militia, whose forces numbered far greater than those of the army.

But in 2003 all that changed. Since the first Gulf War in 1991, Iraq had operated under sanctions imposed by the United Nations that strictly limited the trading that the country could do with other countries. Iraq could not sell its oil in the international market; nor could it receive any goods except medical necessities. Even with black-market trading and the fact that some medical products were allowed under the sanctions, many of the people of Iraq were deprived of lifesaving—and even basic—medical care, as well as food and other products needed to sustain life. Many other Iraqis, especially those favored by the Baath Party, lived very well despite international pressure.

Since the first Gulf War the international community had attempted by various means—sanctions, restrictions, and inspections—to determine if the government of Saddam Hussein was manufacturing what they referred to as weapons of mass destruction.

These weapons were believed to include a variety of poisons that could be spread through the air or water. Although weapons of this sort had been internationally outlawed since World War I, Iraq was known to have used them against Iran and even against its own citizens, the Kurdish people of northern Iraq.

Opposite: **The statue of former president Saddam Hussein stands in front of a destroyed communications center in Baghdad. Throughout Iraq's cities, Iraqis celebrated his overthrow by destroying statues and posters Hussein had installed to honor himself.**

French Foreign Minister Dominique de Villepin, seated next to the Permanent Representative of the People's Republic of China to the United Nations, Wang Yingfan, addresses the United Nations Security Council at the UN headquarters on March 19, 2003. France and China opposed the invasion of Iraq.

TENSION OVER TERRORISM

Repeatedly the United Nations sent inspectors to Iraq to examine manufacturing sites and other places that they believed might be used to make or store weapons of mass destruction. The inspectors failed to find any, and were rarely free to determine their own course of investigation or to speak freely with those who might have had knowledge of the matter.

Inspectors often had reason to suspect that representatives from the Iraqi government were being less than helpful. At times, they found conditions or materials that led them to believe that weapons had been made or stored in the past, but they could not say so with certainty.

The international response to Iraq's level of cooperation was generally negative, but there was disagreement about how much danger Saddam Hussein and his activities posed and, more importantly, what should be done about it. After the terrorist attacks on the United States in September 2001, the administration of U.S. president George W. Bush came to believe that Saddam Hussein posed an intolerable risk. Relying on intelligence that they claimed showed both proof of the presence of weapons of mass destruction and a connection between Afghanistan's al-Qaeda terrorists and the Iraqi regime, the United States urged further inspections.

Finding the results of the inspections and the level of cooperation by the Iraqis unacceptable, the U.S. government prepared for war. Some members of the coalition that had fought the first Gulf War—notably France and Germany—opposed going to war at this time. Throughout the world, people took to the streets to demonstrate their opposition to a new war. Protests in the United States and Great Britain were especially heartfelt.

THE LIFE OF SADDAM HUSSEIN

Saddam Hussein was born on April 28, 1937, in Tikrit, a small, impoverished village 100 miles (161 km) north of Baghdad. He was raised by his mother and a stepfather. He left home to attend secondary school in Baghdad. Having lived in a small village with no electricity or water, Hussein embraced the big city of Baghdad and the political ideas of his uncle, Khairallah Talfah, with whom he lived for several years.

In 1957 the young Hussein joined the little-known but politically active Baath Party and got involved in revolutionary activities. His loyalty was tested when members of the Baath Party instructed him to murder Kassem, the leader of Iraq. Hussein and four others shot Kassem, but did not succeed in killing him. Hussein was forced into exile in Syria and Egypt for several years until Kassem lost power in 1963.

Upon his return to Iraq, Hussein was thrown into prison for attempting to overthrow the government. In 1968 the Baath Party seized power in a coup and Hussein became vice-president and a member of the Revolutionary Command Council. On July 16, 1979, President al-Bakr was forced into resignation by Hussein, who had sufficiently established his power base. Hussein then became president of the Republic of Iraq.

THE SECOND GULF WAR

In spring of 2003, the United States and Great Britain prepared to attack Iraq, with the intention of deposing Saddam Hussein and his Baath Party and destroying his cache of weapons of mass destruction. They called their incursion Operation Iraqi Freedom, referring to the second half of the plan for Iraq—to set up a free and democratic government run by the Iraqi people. By mid-March hundreds of thousands of British, American, and Australian troops had already made their way to Kuwait, where they amassed on Iraq's border, waiting for orders to invade.

The fighting began in the dark hours before dawn on March 19, 2003. Acting on intelligence that told them that Saddam Hussein and his family were hiding in one of his palaces in Baghdad, the United States launched missiles that targeted and bombed the palace and other sites in the city.

An empty street in Baghdad after the second Gulf War. Many Iraqis were afraid to venture out in the evening due to a lack of security and basic services. These shortcomings were very damaging to Iraqi businesses in the city.

The second Gulf War

At the same time, nearly 200,000 coalition forces began their march to Baghdad in a huge cavalry of tanks and armored personnel carriers. Overhead, planes supplied air cover and bombed key sites in the cities.

The first week of the war was eye-opening for the invading forces as well as the ruling regime. The coalition plan was to avoid most of the populated areas in the south of the country, in the belief that the regime had few supporters there. This would greatly lessen civilian casualties and infrastructural damage. The coalition planned to secure as quickly as possible the southern city of Basra and the roads and bridges they would need to move their troops to Baghdad. However, in this endeavor they were met by seemingly unorganized, but fierce, guerrilla opposition. Though initially surprised and slowed, the troops made inexorable progress. On April 3 they took over Saddam International Airport and renamed it Baghdad International Airport. On April 9 they declared themselves in control of Baghdad. For three weeks thousands of bombs and guided missiles fell on Baghdad in an unmistakable demonstration of military supremacy. Resistance from the regime's feared Republican Guard troops stationed around Baghdad never materialized.

Turning their attention to northern Iraq, U.S. Special Forces landed in Kurdish-controlled areas, where, aided by Kurdish militias, they took control of the northern oil fields, barely opposed by the Iraqi army. Now all that remained was Tikrit, Hussein's hometown. On April 14 Tikrit fell to U.S. Marines. Sporadic resistance to coalition forces would continue throughout the country, especially in the cities and former Baathist strongholds, but Bush declared the war to be over.

Throughout the country the Iraqi people took to the streets to celebrate the fall of Hussein and his ruling party. Statues, posters, paintings, and other trappings of his rule were smashed and burned in the streets. In public, most Iraqis celebrated his passing.

"Iraq has no interest in war. No Iraqi official or ordinary citizen has expressed a wish to go to war. The question should be directed at the other side."

—*Saddam Hussein,
February 4, 2003*

Shi'a Muslim men hold a protest outside the Palestine Hotel in Baghdad to demand a larger representation of Shi'a clerics in the new Iraqi government.

THE IRAQI GOVERNMENT AFTER THE WAR

From the beginning of the war, one goal of the invading nations had been to replace Saddam Hussein. To that end, invading forces avoided as much as possible damaging or destroying infrastructure. Nevertheless, at the end of the conflict, the cities were left in disorder. Desperation and anger drove many to loot former palaces of the elite, and even their own institutions and museums. Iraqis who had opposed the regime of Hussein returned from the countries where they had waited out his rule. Some declared themselves political leaders, some religious leaders. But they tended not to remain in power, and there was no clear central government.

After three weeks of fighting, the Baath Party and Hussein and his family appeared to have either fled or died. The invading troops were in possession of Baghdad, and it was time for someone to set up a new government. The United States appointed its own functionaries to supervise restoring infrastructure services, such as electricity, running water, telephone lines, garbage collection, and sewage treatment. They were also in charge of civil security. The Iraqi people were anxious to resume the everyday activities of life: going to school, shopping, banking, and working and conducting business.

Nevertheless, months after the fall of Hussein's regime, much remained to be done to restore order and safety to Iraq. The interim government was not working smoothly. Millions of people had yet to return to work, though the Americans were paying them salaries anyway so they could feed their families. Potential religious and civil leaders rose to prominence almost daily, competing for the loyalties of a confused populace.

Iraqis increasingly resisted the imposition of outside rule and demanded that the United States keep its promise of a free and democratic Iraq. However, the coalition was unable to predict when this would happen or who would emerge to assume leadership as it struggled to balance Iraq's religious, ethnic, and political factions.

These groups were diverse and sometimes operated in opposition to each other. Religious groups included Shi'a Muslims, Sunni Muslims, and Christians. People with ethnic identities and priorities included Arabs, Kurds, Assyrians, and Turkomans. Political contenders included Shi'a-backed groups supporting an Islamic government, as well as secular organizations favoring a democratically elected government and tribal groups, which had traditionally provided order in the rural areas. Into this mix came long-exiled Iraqis, religious and secular, and funding from interests outside Iraq.

As Iraqis struggled to regain their footing in the months following the overthrow of Hussein, the occupying forces found themselves with much to do and no visible end to their responsibility to run Iraq. The Iraqi people looked to their own leaders, to the American administrators, and to themselves for relief, but for everyone the problems were many and the solutions uncertain.

"All the decades of deceit and cruelty have now reached an end. Saddam Hussein and his sons must leave Iraq within 48 hours. Their refusal to do so will result in military conflict, commenced at a time of our choosing."

—*George W. Bush, March 17, 2003*

ECONOMY

WHEN OIL BECAME Iraq's principal industry in the first half of the 20th century, the Iraqi economy surged. Iraq became one of the world's leading producers of oil and earned vast oil revenues. The economy prospered in the 1970s, as oil production rose to its peak toward the end of the 1970s.

In the 1980s the Iraq-Iran War interrupted economic development in Iraq. Oil revenues fell, as oil wells and refineries were destroyed in battle, and the cost of waging war put a great strain on the economy. Iraq spent $35 billion of its reserves financing the eight-year war. By 1988 Iraq had accumulated a debt of $50 billion and the economy hit rock bottom.

After the ceasefire, the oil industry recovered and Iraq's economy picked up. After Iraq invaded Kuwait in 1990, sanctions were imposed restricting Iraqi trade with other nations. This was a devastating blow to the economy, as Iraq depended heavily on oil export revenues.

Left: **Gas fires in the Persian Gulf. Iraq's natural gas reserves account for nearly 20 percent of the world total.**

Opposite: **A coppersmith fashions his wares at his stall in a bazaar.**

After two of Iraq's main export depots were destroyed during the war with Iran, Iraq transported its oil by truck across Turkey and Jordan. Pipelines were subsequently laid between Iraq and Turkey to speed up oil exports.

THE OIL INDUSTRY

The British discovery of oil in Iran in 1908 spurred similar explorations in Iraq. In 1927 the British- and U.S.-controlled Turkish Petroleum Company discovered a rich oil well near the northern city of Kirkuk. The Turkish Petroleum Company was renamed the Iraq Petroleum Company and was granted a 70-year exploration contract by the Iraqi government. By 1938 oil had become Iraq's major export commodity.

After World War II, Basra and Mosul became popular oil-drilling sites. By 1951 Basra, Mosul, and Kirkuk were exporting almost 20 million tons of oil annually. Upset by the revenue earned by foreign companies, the Iraqi government demanded 50 percent of all oil profits.

The Iraq Petroleum Company continued to operate in Iraq until 1973, when the government nationalized the oil companies, paying $300 million for the shares of the Iraq Petroleum Company. The government set up a Ministry of Oil and established the Iraqi National Oil Company, which assumed responsibility for the management of oil production in the country.

Iraq is a member of the Organization of Petroleum Exporting Countries (OPEC), formed in 1960 to control petroleum prices worldwide. In the 1970s OPEC reduced its oil exports, triggering severe oil shortages and skyrocketing oil prices in the United States and other countries that depended on oil imports. OPEC lost some of its influence in the 1980s when attempts to control the world's oil supply failed as countries such as Mexico and the Soviet Union began exporting oil.

Iraq has one of the largest proven oil and natural gas reserves in the world. Its oil reserves are estimated at 112 billion barrels, and its natural gas reserves at 110 trillion cubic feet (3,114,850 million cubic m).

In 1979 Iraqi oil production peaked at 3.5 million barrels per day, but shortly after the invasion of Kuwait, the amount dipped to 300,000 barrels per day. Iraq gradually raised its oil production to two million barrels per day in 2002.

Iraq's main oil fields are located southwest of Basra, near Kirkuk, and northwest of Mosul. Basra was a major oil refining center until its facilities were destroyed in the war with Iran.

IMPACT OF TRADE SANCTIONS

The oil industry is the major source of Iraq's wealth and provides almost all its foreign income. Oil accounts for one-third of the country's gross domestic product and 99 percent of merchandise exports. Iraq's oil revenues finance most government expenditures.

After Iraq's invasion of Kuwait in 1990, the United Nations imposed trade sanctions on Iraq, leading to a decrease in exports of oil and natural gas. Iraq was constrained by trade sanctions and could only import food and medicines approved by the UN. This devastated Iraq's economy and most Iraqis' livelihoods. Smuggling was rife, and consumer products, engineering parts, and machinery were transported by road from Jordan, Turkey, and Syria. However, most merchandise in the market remained beyond the purchasing power of most Iraqis. The sanctions were lifted in 2003 after Saddam Hussein was deposed, but the economy remained in shambles.

AGRICULTURE

Iraq has been an agricultural nation since ancient times. In the 1970s half the Iraqi labor force was engaged in agriculture, but the emphasis on agriculture waned as oil became the primary contributor to the country's economy. Today about 30 percent of Iraqis farm the land, but this figure is falling.

Less than 15 percent of Iraq's land area, mostly in the northeastern plains and mountain valleys, is farmed. The main crops in the delta and plains region are wheat, barley, corn, rice, and fruit. Most of the farmland here is near the Tigris and Euphrates, which provide water for crops. In the northeast, with higher rainfall, tobacco, barley, olives, and fruit are grown. Dates are the largest agricultural export and the second largest foreign currency earner after oil. However, date production fell after the first Gulf War, when oil pollution affected millions of trees in the south.

Before the first Gulf War, Iraq imported 70 percent of its food. Under trade sanctions, food imports were restricted and the agricultural sector raised production but could not meet the demand. As a result, Iraq suffers food shortages.

WATER RESOURCES

For thousands of years, the Tigris and Euphrates rivers have irrigated the land yet also brought destruction. The ancient Sumerian civilization had a myth about these rivers flooding so far that the waters covered large parts of Mesopotamia.

In the last century, Iraq has developed the means to control the flow of the rivers. Several dams in Iraq collect and store floodwater to distribute it to farms during the dry season. The dams bolster Iraq's economy by reducing flood damage, supporting agriculture, and generating electricity.

Workers clear the wheat field at harvest time in northern Iraq.

LAND REFORM

In 1958 the Iraqi government passed a law prohibiting individuals from owning more than 1,000 *dunum* (doo-NOOM), a *dunum* being 10,890 square feet (1,012 square m), of irrigated land or 2,000 *dunum* of rain-watered land. In the 1970s the amount of land an individual was allowed to own was further reduced, and rich farmers were forced to divide their large tracts of land. Many individuals bought small parcels of land and formed collective farms with their neighbors. Collective farms benefited farmers, since they were able to increase their profits while sharing the workload and cost of farming equipment.

REBUILDING BABYLON

Iraq is believed to have 25,000 historic cities, although less than 10 percent have been excavated. One of the most famous was the ancient city of Babylon, which reached the height of its splendor in the sixth and seventh centuries B.C. During the time of Nebuchadnezzar II, Babylon was the largest city in the world, covering about 4 square miles (10 square km). Nebuchadnezzar II lived in a 700-room palace surrounded by the Hanging Gardens of Babylon and a maze of canals. In the center of the ancient city stood the great *ziggurat* of Marduk, the biblical Tower of Babel.

The ruins of Babylon straddle the Euphrates, 55 miles (88.5 km) south of Baghdad. The city had a wide bridge connecting the two banks of the river. It was surrounded by a long thick wall and was guarded by the Ishtar Gate. The wall and the hanging gardens were two of the seven wonders of the ancient world.

Babylon was undergoing restoration works before the 1991 Gulf War, but these efforts were hampered by trade sanctions after the war. The ruins of Babylon did not escape Hussein's legacy; in some sections, the bricks contain an inscription saying that they were laid during the dynasty of Saddam Hussein.

MANUFACTURING

Iraq's manufacturing industries expanded rapidly in the 1970s but declined after the 1991 Gulf War. Besides its oil-related industries, Iraq produces textiles, cement, paper products, and ceramics, and has a food-processing industry using domestic agricultural produce. Most manufactured goods, such as machinery and chemicals, are imported, but until 2003 sanctions have severely limited such imports. Almost all Iraq's factories are located in the cities, especially Baghdad.

TRANSPORTATION

Fishing thrives along the Tigris and Euphrates and supplies the local food-processing industry.

During the 1980s the government invested large sums to improve the transportation system. Winding dirt roads linking the major cities became modern express highways, the lifeline for the transportation of oil.

Iraq's two modern international airports are in Baghdad and Basra. The state airline is Iraqi Airways. Saddam International Airport in Baghdad was renamed Baghdad International Airport after the 2003 Gulf War.

The railway system of Iraq was very primitive until the 1960s—a standard gauge line ran from Baghdad to the Syrian border, and a meter gauge line linked Baghdad to Basra. (Gauge measures the width of the railway line.) The incompatibility of the two lines was a great hindrance in transporting cargo. After extensive work, with funding from the former Soviet Union, Iraq's improved railroad runs from Basra to Baghdad, Mosul, Kirkuk, Syria, and Turkey.

ENVIRONMENT

IRAQ'S ENVIRONMENT has deteriorated drastically in the last two decades. One of the main direct causes of environmental damage in the country has been war: an eight-year war with Iran during the 1980s, followed in 1991 by the Gulf War. Iraq is suffering the consequences of the policies of Saddam Hussein's dictatorship and of a 12-year trade embargo. Iraq's political and economic environment has resulted in severe damage to the natural environment. This in turn has adversely affected the people and wildlife of Iraq.

NATURE, A VICTIM OF WAR

While the loss of human life is usually the most painful consequence of war, the loss of plant and animal life due to war also has serious implications. Iraq's terrain consists mainly of desert, mountains, and marshlands. Located in the northern part of the gulf, the country is an important area for migratory and endemic birds, including around 15 threatened species. Iraq's birdlife includes the greater flamingo, white-headed duck, and Basra reed warbler, which is native to Iraq.

The war with Iran from 1980 to 1988 polluted marshlands where wetland birds spend winter. During the first Gulf War, following Iraq's invasion of Kuwait, allied bombing and tank tracking destroyed great expanses of vegetation in the Iraqi desert. Millions of barrels of crude oil spilled into the Persian Gulf blackened surrounding coasts and killed marine life.

The short war in 1991 generated long-term environmental damage, but before the land could recover from its effects, in 2003 a second Gulf War erupted. The legacy of war in Iraq is likely to intensify, unless radioactive waste from the use of depleted uranium ammunition is disposed of properly.

A SCARRED LAND

During Iraq's years of war, some of the most severely damaged landscapes have been the southern marshlands between the Tigris and Euphrates rivers. The number of marsh Arabs, who have farmed and fished in these marshlands for centuries, dwindled substantially under Saddam Hussein's regime—from the hundreds of thousands in the mid-1900s to the tens of thousands at the start of the 21st century.

After the first Gulf War, Hussein built large dams and canals in the marshlands, which drained large sections of the marshes and left the land parched. Hussein also launched a brutal campaign to drive political opponents out of the marshlands, and as a result many marsh Arabs fled from their homes to Iran. Those who remained in Iraq were scattered in camps around the country. There is no way they can return to the dried-up marshlands, which are no longer able to support life. The traditional way of life of the marsh Arabs has been virtually destroyed.

Besides the desiccation of the marshlands, desertification is another adverse effect of war on the land. Military activity speeds up the process of desert expansion. Tank tracks and bomb explosions crush and burn desert flora

and pollute the sands with oil and debris, while toxins released from weapons of war poison groundwater.

During the first Gulf War, the allied forces hit water and sewage treatment plants in Iraq. As a result, the Iraqis were deprived of clean drinking water, and waste water and garbage flooded the streets. Such conditions led to outbreaks of waterborne diseases, such as typhoid, from which thousands suffered and died.

After more than a decade of sanctions, even as the second Gulf War loomed, Baghdad's water and sewage treatment facilities were still in a poor state, and some streets were still blocked and flooded.

Buildings, including schools and homes, and environmental and archeological sites were destroyed during the 2003 Gulf War. A lack of finances and a glut of social and health problems hindered repairs in the 1990s. Even with a new regime, sanctions and debts (to Iran and Kuwait for damage caused in the 1980s and in 1991) will impede the healing of this deeply scarred land.

Above: **The ruins of a building in Abul Khasib, south of Basra, after the Gulf War.**

Opposite: **A boy stands in a garbage-filled street, a picture of post-war devastation.**

SHRINKING MARSHLANDS

Iraq's marshlands are located between the Tigris and the Euphrates, before the rivers flow into the Persian Gulf. The valley was the site of ancient Mesopotamia, and it is believed by many to be the location of the biblical Garden of Eden.

Iraq's marshlands have supported human communities and wildlife for 5,000 years. Today the marshlands are one of the most important wetland areas in the world. The marshlands are a wintering stop for migratory birds and a breeding spot for endemic fauna, some of which have become extinct with the shrinking of their natural habitat. Since the 1970s Iraq's marshlands, the largest wetlands in the Middle East, have shrunk from 7,700 square miles (20,000 square km) to less than 770 square miles (2,000 square km)—a more than 90 percent reduction in size.

The main cause of the dessication of the marshlands has been the construction of more than 30 large dams over 40 years and of massive drainage works after the 1991 Gulf War. The dams and the drainage works have caused the marshes to dry up, leaving behind cracked earth.

Less than 10 percent of the original marshlands have survived Hussein's destructive projects. The only hope for the remaining marshlands (*below*) and their fragile ecosystem is for the new regime in Iraq to take strong conservation measures and to implement programs to reflood the marshes. To do this, Iraq will need financial and technological support from the international community.

OIL SPILLS

In 1991, as Iraqi soldiers retreated from Kuwait, they released millions of barrels of crude oil into the Persian Gulf to hold off coalition forces. The oil blackened the gulf coast, staining beaches not just in Kuwait but in neighboring nations as well. The oil poisoned or suffocated thousands of fish and waterbirds, and it was predicted that toxins from oil residues might continue to affect fisheries in the gulf for a hundred years.

With help from its neighbors and from the United States and other nations, the Kuwaiti government spent millions of dollars cleaning up after the oil spills. As the second gulf war loomed in 2003, pollution-control companies went on the alert to organize cleanup crews in the event of a similar ecological disaster. Since heavy machinery might do more damage to the beaches, workers would be hired to shovel oil out of affected areas.

As in 1991, the United States sent coastguard cutters and jets to the Persian Gulf in 2003 to monitor oil movements in the event of a spill.

Oil pumped into the sea during the Gulf War is washed onto a beach in Saudi Arabia.

Opposite: **Depleted uranium (DU) ammunition used in Iraq during the Gulf War.**

OIL FIRES

Oil fires have been a major source of air pollution in Iraq. In 1991 Iraqi troops set oil wells in Kuwait on fire as they retreated. Firefighters took months after the war to stop the fires, which filled the skies over Iraq as well as Kuwait and Saudi Arabia with soot and other toxic particles. The airborne pollutants mixed with water vapor and formed clouds of acid rain. The oil fires also produced high levels of carbon dioxide, with possible climate change consequences. (Carbon dioxide contributes to the greenhouse effect in the atmosphere.) Massive cleanup efforts lasted a decade, but the oil fires, oil mists, and acid rains had already done irreversible damage to the air, causing respiratory problems among people and poisoning plants and animals.

The potential environmental impact of oil fires in 2003 raised even more concern, because the second Gulf War would take place inside a substantially larger country dotted with many more oil wells across its varied terrain. Kirkuk, one of Iraq's largest oil fields, was an especially worrying spot, because the oil there contained a high level of sulfur.

HEALTH MATTERS

Iraq's environmental issues are also major health issues. For example, without proper sanitation and clean water, many Iraqis have contracted life-threatening diseases, which the hospitals are unable to treat without adequate and appropriate medical supplies. Certain diseases resulting from unclean drinking water and poor sanitation cause malnutrition among children. For example, sufferers of dysentery are unable to retain food and absorb essential nutrients.

The hospitals are even less equipped to treat patients during wartime, when there are more and worse cases, such as severe burns, because access to medical and surgical supplies is more difficult on the battlefield.

Land near the Iraq-Iran border is plagued with landmines laid in the 1980s that did not explode during the war and still lie in the earth like ticking time bombs. For Iraqis living near the border, stepping on a landmine is a daily possibility. Landmines in Iraq have maimed or killed many people, such as Bedouin nomads. Landmines have also killed animals.

Since the 1991 war in the Persian Gulf, there have been claims that radioactive dust from depleted uranium munitions is the cause of severe defects and deformities in babies born after the war. Chemical and biological weapons have been blamed for a higher incidence of cancer and for chronic illnesses, such as the Gulf War Syndrome, among Iraqi civilians and U.S. war veterans.

Aid organizations such as Doctors Without Borders and Save the Children have brought volunteer professionals to help local doctors. As damage and health assessments reveal the effects of the wars on the Iraqi people, the most urgent efforts to repair and restore the environment include cleaning up oil-polluted areas, repairing water and sewage treatment facilities, and properly disposing of hazardous metals from detonated war weapons.

IRAQIS

IRAQIS COME FROM diverse ethnic backgrounds. Mesopotamian history counts conquerors and immigrants as part of the people of the land between the rivers. Today more than three-quarters of Iraqis are Arabs, at least 15 percent are Kurds, and the rest include Turkomans, Persians, and Assyrians.

There is tension between certain ethnic groups, such as the Arabs and the Kurds. Iraq has a large Kurdish minority, but under Saddam Hussein Kurds suffered a lack of political rights for decades. After the 1991 Gulf War, many Kurds left Iraq to escape Hussein's program of ethnic cleansing. Kurdish hopes for their own independent state centered on Kirkuk, where most Iraqi Kurds live, remained unfulfilled after the 2003 Gulf War. Even as displaced Kurds tried to return, Kurdish fighters were forced to leave the city.

Another area of ethnic tension is between the Arabs in Iraq and the Iranians. Until 1980 a number of Iranians were living in Iraq, but during the Iraq-Iran War some Iranians in Iraq were killed while others were driven back to Iran.

Iraqi Arabs are themselves fragmented along religious lines, between Shi'a and Sunni Muslims. The 2003 Gulf War raised hopes among the largely Shi'a population for more rights after decades of discrimination and persecution by Hussein's largely Sunni government.

Above: **The reed houses of Iraq's marsh Arabs. Reed houses have been built in Iraq since the time of the early Sumerians.**

Opposite: **A Muslim Iraqi fingers prayer beads as he leans against a tiled panel outside the Al Kufa Mosque.**

51

THE ARABS

Iraq is part of the Arab world, which stretches from Iraq and Syria downward to Sudan and Somalia, and from Oman and the United Arab Emirates westward to Morocco and Mauritania in northern Africa. Most Iraqis are Arabs who speak Arabic and follow the Islamic faith.

HISTORY The Arab people originated in the Arabian peninsula, which was separated from the rest of the ancient world by the sea on three sides and by the Euphrates river and the great desert in the north.

The ancient Arabs lived in small clans consisting of several families. The clans were constantly at war with one another and raided one another's villages. The Arabs were aggressive and considered it honorable to die in battle. Acts of vengeance for the death of clan members were common.

In the seventh century, the Arabs began converting to Islam. They helped Prophet Muhammad to spread Islam in the Middle East. In so doing, the Arabs settled in new lands, where they drove out nonbelievers. In a short span of time, the Arabs became the primary inhabitants of Iraq and other countries in the Middle East and northern Africa.

THE BEDOUIN The Bedouin are an Arab people that have recently begun making a transition from their traditional nomadic lifestyle to living as settled farmers. There are still nomadic Bedouin living out of portable tents in the desert, roaming in search of grazing land for their livestock.

In the 1860s Bedouin made up more than 30 percent of Iraq's population; today they are less than 1 percent. Many Bedouin live in the neutral zone between Iraq and Saudi Arabia.

MODERN ARABS Iraqi Arabs strongly believe in religion, tradition, and family. Families are closeknit, and elders are highly respected. Traditionally, Arabs are very generous to strangers and very supportive of friends, with whom they form lasting bonds.

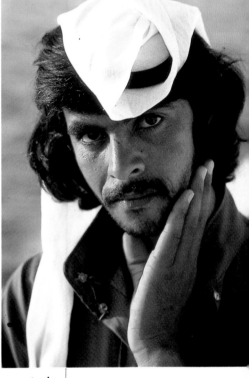

Above: **An Iraqi man with his headcloth blown by the wind.**

Opposite: **Iraqi beauty borne of ethnic fusion in a country between Arabia and Persia.**

There are conflicts, such as a growing economic disparity among Arab countries—between those, such as Kuwait, that have grown rich on oil exports, and the less wealthy, such as Iraq. Despite having the second largest oil reserves in the world, most Iraqis are extremely poor because of dictatorship, war, and sanctions.

Economic disparities in the Arab world and within Arab countries have raised discontent over several issues among poorer Arabs. These issues include the lack of trade and joint ventures between Arab nations, the lavish spending by the richer states on ostentatious airports and palaces, and the plight of the Palestinians.

OTHER MINORITIES

Apart from the Kurds, there are other, smaller minority groups in Iraq. These include the Turkomans, the Assyrians and Armenians, and the Persians.

The Turkomans make up around 3 percent of the Iraqi population. They speak a Turkish dialect and are Sunni Muslims. They live in villages around Mosul and Kirkuk in the northeast.

The Assyrians are descendants of the ancient Mesopotamians. They speak Aramaic and are Christians. They live in northeastern Iraq and belong to the middle- and upper-class social brackets. The Armenians live mainly in Baghdad and are also Christians. Many came as traders in the early 17th century during the Ottoman-Persian wars.

The Persians of Iraq live mainly in Karbala, An Najaf, and Samarra.

SOCIAL SYSTEM

Iraqi society consists of three main classes: upper, middle, and lower. A person's social status is usually determined by birth, but the class system does allow for a degree of upward mobility.

UPPER CLASS Members of the Iraqi upper class include government officials, wealthy people with distinguished ancestors, and influential individuals. Wealth is not a guarantee of upper-class status. In addition to being rich, Iraqis must have a good family name or hold an important position to be considered upper-class citizens.

MIDDLE CLASS Teachers, military personnel, government employees, small landowners, and businesspeople are among those who make up the Iraqi middle class. They are usually college-educated, moderately wealthy, and live in cities.

More Iraqis moved up into the middle-class social bracket during the 1970s and the 1980s when the government made available more opportunities for education.

LOWER CLASS Iraq's lower class consists of farmers, rural workers, manual laborers, and the unemployed. Iraqis do not place a stigma on members of the lower class. Although this class does not mix with the upper class, there is very little tension between the groups.

DRESS

Generally, Iraqis in the cities dress Western-style, while rural Iraqis still dress in traditional Arab attire.

TRADITIONAL MENSWEAR Men in Iraq traditionally wear the *thobe* (THOH-bay), an ankle-length caftan with long sleeves. In the past, men wore colorful caftans, but today these are plain. This roomy garment allows air to circulate inside, which helps to cool the body in the heat of the desert.

A light cotton caftan, usually white, is preferred during summer because it is cool. In winter men wear caftans of heavier fabric, such as wool, in darker shades of grey or black. Another gown may be worn over the *thobe* for added warmth.

One of the most distinguishing features of the traditional Iraqi man's attire is the headcloth, called a *kaffiyeh* (kah-fee-YEH) in central and northern Iraq, and a *gutra* (GOO-trah) in the south. The headcloth is a square piece of cloth that is folded to form a triangle. It is usually made from cotton or wool, and is commonly plain white or checkered red.

Worn over a skull cap, the headcloth may be twisted around the top of the head like a turban, or draped over the head like a flowing veil. It is often held in place by an *igaal* (ee-GAAL), a twisted, black, rope-like coil that circles the top of the head like a wreath.

More than a decorative piece, the *kaffiyeh*, or *gutra*, has a practical use—it protects Iraqi men from the sun's rays and the night cold. Bedouin men who live in the open desert find the headcloth especially useful in sandstorms, as they can pull the cloth over the mouth and nose to keep out the fine airborne sand.

Kurdish men wear Western-style clothes most of the time. They wear their traditional clothes during special occasions such as weddings and festivals.

Traditional Kurdish menswear usually consists of a pair of baggy wide pants called pantaloons, secured by a cummerbund sash around the waist; a skull cap; and a fringed turban in red checks, blue, brown, or white. In winter, Kurdish men wear woolen turbans, and they may wear one long-sleeved shirt over another, or a vest over a shirt.

A face veil safeguards a woman's modesty and shades her face from the sun and sand.

TRADITIONAL WOMEN'S WEAR Iraqi women wear a dark-colored cloak called *abaaya* (ah-BAH-yah) that covers the body from head to ankle except for the face. The plain, bulky *abaaya* may appear like a uniform but for the individual's personal touches. For a start, the fabric used for each *abaaya* varies in shade and texture.

In addition, younger women often decorate their cloaks with gold-colored embroidery or bright-colored fringes, while wealthier women belt their *abaaya* with a wide, jeweled girdle. A dress is worn under the *abaaya*.

Unlike in certain other Arab nations, in Iraq women are not required by law or custom to veil themselves in public, although they may if they choose to. Many of the modern, educated women in Iraq's cities have switched from traditional Arab to Western-style dress. But for women in Iraq's rural towns, the *abaaya* is essential for modesty.

Many women in the rural areas also wear a face veil, a practice that began in the Middle East as far back as 1500 B.C. These women cannot accept the thought of leaving their arms, legs, or face exposed when they leave the house and are shocked by the boldness of urban women who go out in public without the safety of the *abaaya*.

Traditional Kurdish women's wear consists of two layers, one long, bright-colored dress over another. In addition, Muslim Kurdish women wear a headscarf. Like Kurdish men, Kurdish women wear Western-style clothes, reserving their traditional clothes for special occasions.

Dressed in *abaaya*, two rural Iraqi women wait for a bus to the city.

LIFESTYLE

THE LIFESTYLE OF IRAQIS is determined and molded by their basic values and beliefs. One of the most important values is family loyalty. The family is a cohesive social unit that nurtures its young and old alike. Iraqis also greatly value a person's honor and dignity, and take all efforts to maintain an honorable reputation. Central beliefs held by all Iraqis include the ultimate controlling nature of fate, differences between men and women, and the increase of wisdom with age.

Iraqis are generous and loyal people. They are very polite to friends, who are also expected to fulfill certain duties. If a friend asks a favor, it is considered very rude to turn him or her down.

A stranger is not given the same consideration as a friend, which may cause Iraqis to appear rude to foreigners. Once personal contact is made, however, Iraqis change their manner and become very accommodating and pleasant.

Left: **Water is scarce in the dry and arid regions of western Iraq. Water tankers make regular stops to ensure a dependable water supply for the people who live there.**

Opposite: **A young man herding camels in Iraq.**

63

FAMILY LIFE

The family is the most important social unit in Iraqi society. Iraqis consider it a disgrace to speak badly of family members or to talk to outsiders about family problems.

An Iraqi family consists of all related kin, which can include hundreds of people. Most Iraqis feel a strong affiliation to their relatives and make conscious efforts to maintain close family ties. Iraqis cherish their children and place their family above everything else.

RURAL FAMILIES The typical rural household consists of the eldest son and his parents, wife, and children. Sisters, brothers, cousins, aunts, uncles, and grandparents live in neighboring homes. Close geographical proximity allows Iraqi children to learn meaningful values and beliefs from their relatives.

URBAN FAMILIES As younger Iraqis migrate to the cities, they leave their older family members behind. In the cities, families do not always live together. But despite the distance between them, Iraqis are delighted to provide shelter or financial support for relatives in need. They know that when they are in trouble, other relatives will likewise extend a helping hand.

ROLES In a traditional Iraqi family, each member has a clearly defined role. Children are expected to respect and obey their parents and grandparents, while grandparents offer advice and depend on their children to take care of them.

The mother traditionally serves as the loving and compassionate figure in the household. She is expected to care for both her children and her parents as well as look after the household, but she has limited influence in decisions.

The father is traditionally recognized as the head of the family. He is the disciplinarian and figure of authority.

LINEAGE Iraqis, especially those in the upper and middle classes, are proud of their ancestral lineage. A family high up the social ladder uses its status to secure high-paying jobs and attract influential friends.

Lower-class Iraqis also take pride in their family name and try to prevent their family's reputation from being tarnished.

Above: **A fish vendor tends to his customers. As the head of the family, an Iraqi man may be the sole breadwinner.**

Opposite: **A mother holds her child in her arms while attending a class.**

Kurdish women in colorful dresses with intricate embroidery.

MARRIAGE

Most Iraqi marriages are arranged by the family. Several things are taken into account for marriage, such as the potential partner's character, background, and financial position. Once two families decide upon a marriage, the man and woman meet and become acquainted. If either is dissatisfied with the match, the marriage is cancelled. More and more young, educated Iraqis in the cities are choosing their own partners, although they still seek their parents' approval.

In rural areas, marriages between first or second cousins are fairly common, particularly among tribal communities. Such marriages barely exist in the cities. Tribes arrange marriages between relatives because they can confidently judge the background and character of the bride and groom and keep money and property within the family.

Until a few decades ago, when polygamy was outlawed in Iraq, men married more than one woman. Muslim men can have up to four wives at a time, but this is discouraged in Iraq, where men have to apply for permission in court to have more than one wife.

Marriages in Iraq are based on financial security and companionship. For unsuccessful marriages, divorce is permissible by Islamic law. Both men and women must obtain a divorce through court proceedings, although it is easier for a man to obtain a divorce.

An Iraqi man must pay his divorced wife enough money to support herself and her children. Both parties can remarry without any stigma attached to them. Children of divorced parents normally live with their mother until they are 7 to 9 years old. After age 9, they are allowed to choose with whom they want to live.

An Iraqi Kurdish wedding couple.

Women at the Baghdad Technical College. Women make up 25 percent of the Iraqi labor force.

PROPER SOCIAL BEHAVIOR

Men's and women's roles in Iraqi society have changed in recent years. Women have been given more freedom than before, largely because of the eight-year war with Iran and the 1991 Gulf War. As men left their jobs to join the armed forces and fight in the wars, professions in law, medicine, and business were open to women for the first time. Iraqi law approved the status of professional women because there were not enough men to fill the vacant positions.

Although women have joined men in the labor force, there are still clearly defined social behaviors for each of the sexes. Men and women, even husbands and wives, are segregated in public. When friends get together, the sexes usually divide among themselves. It is considered improper for an unmarried man and an unmarried woman to be alone together. Even men and women who work together avoid sustained contact with the opposite sex. Traditional Iraqis prefer this norm of gender separation, finding that they feel more comfortable in social settings this way. Platonic friendships between a man and a woman are rarely heard of in Iraqi society.

In rural areas, men and women follow the traditional social norms. Women rarely leave the house except to visit friends. It is considered improper for a woman to be seen in public without her veil or to shop in the market. An unmarried woman's reputation is ruined if she is seen with a man.

Men and women in rural areas are completely segregated. Even married couples rarely spend time together except while sleeping and eating. Men work and spend their leisure time in the company of other men. Women spend their time raising children, cooking, weaving, and socializing with friends.

Two Iraqi professional women.

Iraqi children have grown up in an environment of uncertainty and instability for decades.

CHILDREN

Iraqi parents love and cherish their children, yet raise them with strict discipline. The young are taught from an early age the importance of honoring and respecting the elder members of society.

Unlike children in the United States, children in Iraq usually live with their parents until they marry. Often, young adults choose to continue living with their parents even after marriage. If a newly married couple moves out of their parents' home, their parents will help decorate and finance their new home.

Alongside lessons in love and security, discipline is inculcated at an early age. Bad behavior will not go unpunished, and the child is warned to never repeat the act. Parents tend not to reason with their children or try to rationalize their misbehavior.

Iraqi children grow up with their siblings and cousins. The adults in their life include parents, grandparents, aunts, and uncles. The cohesive nature of Iraqi families shows children the strength of the family unit.

The suffering of Iraqi babies and children can only have fueled Iraqis' love for their children. Wars and trade sanctions have subjected children to physical, emotional, and psychological pain. Many have died from malnutrition or bodily injuries, but those who survive have been scarred for life by memories of losing their homes and loved ones to war.

EDUCATION

Iraq's education system has three levels: primary, secondary, and college.

Iraqi youth receive their elementary education between ages 6 and 12 and attend secondary school between ages 12 and 18. During the last three years of secondary school, students are allowed to choose between college preparatory classes or vocational school. Students in vocational schools learn trade skills in agriculture, industry, home economics, and commerce.

A group of students meet in the campus of the University of Mustansiriyah in Baghdad.

Colleges and universities offer the highest level of education in Iraq. There are several public universities, including four in Baghdad and others in Basra, Mosul, Arbil, Tikrit, Al-Kufah, Al-Qadisiyah, and Al-Anbar.

The quality of education in Iraq improved dramatically after the 1958 revolution. Education was provided free by the government up to college level. Before 1991 Iraq had one of the best education systems in the region, with a 100-percent enrollment rate in primary schools and high levels of literacy among both men and women.

However, more than a decade of trade sanctions following the 1991 Gulf War resulted in reduced public expenditure on education. No new schools have been built, while existing ones are overcrowded and degenerated, lacking electricity, sanitation, and teaching equipment. Many children have dropped out of school to help support their family, and literacy rates have fallen, especially among women. Rebuilding Iraq's education system and infrastructure will be a major priority and challenge for the new administration in Iraq.

CITY LIFE

In the past 60 years, there has been a widespread migration of Iraqis to urban centers. The Basra and Al-Qadisiyah regions recorded the greatest movement of rural population to cities.

These waves of migration have had an interesting effect. Iraq's urbanites were once a collection of individuals who left home to start a new life. Today the cities are filled with neighborhoods of friends and relatives, and this has made the cities warmer and friendlier.

During an economic slump in the 1950s, Iraqis were forced to build mud homes and live in crowded shantytowns. The government began to subsidize housing projects to accomodate the growing population.

During the gulf wars, many families left Baghdad for the countryside further north to escape allied bombing.

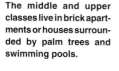

The middle and upper classes live in brick apartments or houses surrounded by palm trees and swimming pools.

RURAL LIFE

Iraq's villages consist of families that make up a tribe. The village tribe is usually governed by a sheikh, who lives in the largest house. The tribe includes resident tradesmen and government officials.

Villagers live in small houses made of mud bricks. Their customs are deeply rooted in tradition. In most households, elderly parents live with their eldest son and his family. Other family members live in nearby houses in the village.

Parents prefer to send their children to religious schools. Children follow in their parents' footsteps in choosing a career. For instance, the son of a blacksmith usually becomes a blacksmith.

Since the villages' economic base is agriculture, most villages lie on the banks of the Tigris or Euphrates. Water from the rivers is pumped to the villages by primitive means to irrigate the farms. Agriculture and raising livestock are the main occupations of villagers.

The traditional mud huts of Iraqi villages have thatched roofs of twigs or reeds. The dirt floors are covered with woven rugs. Electricity, clean water, and other amenities are becoming a part of Iraqi village life.

RELIGION

RELIGION IS ONE of the most important aspects of life in Iraq. Almost everyone in Iraq feels strongly about their faith, especially because they have experienced so much poverty and pain. In times of relative peace, those perceived as not leading a religious life are often shunned by their neighbors. Atheists and agnostics are not easily accepted.

Iraqis try to pray and practice their religion daily. Religion pervaded many activities in relatively peaceful times. It was taught in classrooms; it dictated marriage and divorce laws; and it often played a part in business and banking. Until the Baath Party took over in the 1960s, the mosque and the state were united. While the Baath Party recognized Islam as the official religion, it set up a secular government.

About 95 percent of the people are Muslims; they are divided into two sects: Shi'a (SHEE-a) or Sunni (SOON-nee). Shi'a and Sunni Muslims differ in some of their practices. Shi'a Muslims make up 53 percent of the population, Sunni Muslims 42 percent.

The rest of the population are either Christians or Jews. In the West's fight against global terrorism, Christians have faced persecution in Iraq due to their perceived connection to the West.

Opposite: **Friday noon prayers at a mosque.**

Below: **The golden dome of the al-Abbas Mosque in Karbala is a holy shrine for Shi'a Muslims.**

MESOPOTAMIA UNITED

Mesopotamia had as many religions as there were ethnic groups. Each invasion and change of rule introduced a new religion to Mesopotamia. In 588 or 587 B.C. the Chaldean king Nebuchadnezzar II destroyed Jerusalem and exiled thousands of Jews in Babylon. Many Jews later fled from Mesopotamia to escape persecution when the Mesopotamians adopted the religious beliefs of the new conquerors.

Islam came to the region in A.D. 637 when the Arab Muslims defeated the Iranian Sassanids. The majority of the population became Muslims, including the Kurds. Mass arrivals of Arabs from Oman and eastern Arabia bolstered the Mesopotamian Muslim population. Small Christian and Jewish communities retained their faith and remained in Mesopotamia.

Until the coming of Islam, Mesopotamia was a collage of different religions. People worshiped the gods of their tribes and families. The teachings of Prophet Muhammad gathered the multireligious people under one faith.

SHI'A AND SUNNI MUSLIMS

After the death of Muhammad, Muslims disagreed on who would be his successor, or caliph. One group chose Abu Bakar al-Siddiq, a close and faithful associate of Muhammad. Al-Siddiq was succeeded by Umar bin al-Khatab and Uthman bin Affan before insurgencies arose.

A section of the Muslim population believed that Ali bin Abi Talib, the prophet's son-in-law, deserved the caliphate since he was a direct descendant of the prophet. This group founded the Shi'a sect of Islam. The majority, who practice the traditions and way of life of Prophet Muhammad, or *sunnah* (SOON-nah), belong to the Sunni sect.

Despite similar beliefs about the teachings of Muhammad and the Koran, there is a political divide between the two sects in Iraq. Shi'a Muslims in Iraq feel that the Sunni minority, which held political power under Saddam Hussein, have subjected the Shi'a majority to unfair discrimination. The end of Hussein's rule in 2003 offered Shi'a Muslims and other religious groups hope for a chance to determine their future.

The Kadhimain Mosque in Baghdad is a holy shrine for Shi'a Muslims.

JOURNEY TO MECCA

The hajj occurs in Zulhijjah, the last month of the Islamic lunar calendar, more exactly between 8 and 13 Zulhijjah. The pilgrims conduct rites such as the following:

- Wearing a white seamless garment. This symbolizes purity and the equality of every person in the eyes of God.
- Standing at the plain of 'Arafat. This reminds pilgrims of the Day of Judgment.
- Collecting small pebbles at Mudzalifah and throwing them at white pillars in Mina. This reenacts Abraham's efforts to chase away Satan, who tempted him to disobey God.
- Sacrificing a goat or sheep. This commemorates how God, in appreciation of Abraham's steadfastness, replaced Abraham's son with a sheep at the time of the sacrifice.
- Walking seven times around the Ka'bah, a cube-like monument built by Abraham that sits in the Grand Mosque (*above*).
- Kissing or touching the Black Stone in the Ka'bah. Prophet Muhammad kissed the stone when he made his pilgrimage. Muslims believe that the stone was light-colored and shining when the angel Gabriel brought it from heaven and that it became black with the sins of humankind.
- Running seven times between the Safa and Marwa hills. This recalls Hagar's frantic attempts to find water for her baby, Ishmael.

CHARITY Every Muslim who has the means is expected to give money to the less fortunate every year at the end of the fast of Ramadan. One of the reasons for this is so that the poor and needy can join in the Eid al-Fitr celebration. In addition, wealthy Muslims are expected to give to charity whenever their possessions meet certain conditions. This is for the general good and prosperity of society, to prevent poverty. It also keeps selfishness and greed at bay.

FASTING During the month of Ramadan, Muslims fast and abstain from food, drink, and sex daily from dawn to dusk. They must also avoid futile activities such as lying or harming others. Fighting during the Iraq-Iran War stopped for the holy month of Ramadan.

Fasting helps Muslims understand the plight of the poor and hungry and to be more willing to extend a helping hand. It trains Muslims to be patient, disciplined, and compassionate, while removing base desires such as greed and an excessive love for material things. Fasting is also beneficial to health and weight management. Above all, Muslims fast to bring themselves closer to God.

Almost all Muslims fast during the month of Ramadan; exceptions are very young children, the sick, the old, and women who are pregnant, breastfeeding, or menstruating.

PILGRIMAGE Muslims are expected to make the pilgrimage, or hajj, to the holy city of Mecca at least once in their lives, if they can afford to. Every year, more than two million Muslims from countries all over the world gather in Mecca for the hajj.

Muslims believe that a successful pilgrimage cleanses them from all their previous sins, making them as pure as newborns by the time they go back home.

CHRISTIANS AND JEWS

Christians make up the largest non-Muslim group in Iraq. Many Iraqi Christians are Assyrian Christians, or Nestorians. The Nestorians broke away from the Roman Catholic Church in the fifth century due to a doctrinal disagreement, and founded their own church. But the largest church in Iraq is the Chaldean Church, established in the 16th century when some Nestorians reunited with the Roman Catholic Church in doctrine but kept their Eastern rite practices in worship.

Sunday is the universal Christian holy day, when all Christians attend church to worship God as a community. Sunday is a day of rest, when many Christian businesses and shops in Iraq's cities close.

Jews have lived in Iraq since Mesopotamian times. Throughout their history, Iraqi Jews have suffered persecution and displacement. Mob attacks in the 1940s injured or killed many Jews in Iraq. In the years following the birth of the state of Israel in 1948, Operations Ezra and Nechemia saw more than 100,000 Jews leave Iraq for Israel. More Jews left Iraq after emigration restrictions were lifted in the early 1970s, and today there are as few as 100 Jews left in Iraq.

RELIGIOUS LEGACY Several stories from the bible have been linked to places in Iraq. Abraham, the patriarch of the Jews, was born in Ur, an ancient city in southern Iraq. The prophet Daniel was thrown into the furnace of Nebuchadnezzar's palace in Babylon and was unharmed because he was a believer of God. Many also believe that the Garden of Eden, where Adam and Eve lived before their fall into sin, is in a village called Al-Qurna, some 46 miles (74 km) north of Basra where the Tigris and Euphrates rivers meet. Adam supposedly first spoke to God at a eucalyptus tree in Al-Qurna known as Adam's Tree.

THE KORAN AND THE BIBLE

Among the major world religions, Islam, Christianity, and Judaism are most closely related. There are distinct differences among the three faiths, but also notable similarities.

Christianity and Judaism share the books of the Old Testament in the Christian Bible. Islam and Christianity share several beliefs, including the existence of both heaven and hell; the birth of Jesus Christ to a virgin, Mary; and Jesus's ability to perform miracles.

Both the Koran (*above, a chapter from the Koran*) and the Bible describe the story of the creation of the human race in the first man and woman, Adam and Eve. Both holy books emphasize the importance of faith in God and talk about the Day of Judgment. Both faiths share prophets such as Adam, Noah, Abraham, and Moses.

However, a major difference between Islam and Christianity, perhaps the most significant difference, is the identity of Jesus. While Muslims believe that Jesus was merely a prophet, Christians believe that he was the son of God made flesh, God and man at the same time.

Nonetheless, Muslims believe that Islam belongs to the same root of faith as do Christianity and Judaism. Indeed, a close comparison of the Koran, the Bible, and the Tanakh reveal the common foundations on which the three faiths are built.

LANGUAGE

THE OFFICIAL LANGUAGE of Iraq is Arabic, which is also the official language of the Middle Eastern Arab nations and the language of Islam.

The minority groups in Iraq speak some Arabic in addition to their mother tongue, such as Armenian, Kurdish, Syriac, or Turkish.

Iraq's Armenians, mostly in Baghdad, Basra, and Mosul, speak the official language of Armenia. There are also Armenian speakers in other Middle Eastern nations, the United States, and the former Soviet Union.

Kurdish is the largest minority language spoken in Iraq and is also spoken in Turkey, Iran, Syria, and Armenia. Kurdish is written in Roman, Arabic, and Cyrillic scripts.

The Assyrians, in northern Iraq, speak Syriac, which is a dialect of Aramaic, believed to be the language of Jesus Christ and his Apostles.

The Turkomans speak a Turkish dialect that is related to languages spoken in Central Asia and Mongolia.

Left: **Cuneiform is the earliest evidence of written language. The Sumerians printed these shapes in wet clay. Historians believe that Mesopotamia was the world's first civilization to explore writing.**

Opposite: **Iraqi Kurds at a newsstand in downtown Arbil.**

A title page of the Koran in beautiful Arabic calligraphy. The script lends itself to a form of calligraphy that transforms ordinary writing into an exquisite art form.

WRITTEN ARABIC

Written Arabic did not exist in the early days of the language; the early Arabs depended on oral means of communication. Arabic script was derived from the Aramaic Nabataean alphabet and was used extensively in the fifth century. The Arabs gradually improved the Arabic script and produced a beautiful form of calligraphy, which the Arabs used to write thousands of copies of their holy book, the Koran.

ARABIC

Arabic, one of the major languages of the world and the sixth official language of the United Nations, is the sacred language of Islam. Arabic originated in Saudi Arabia before the fifth century B.C. Prophet Muhammad preached in Arabic, and the language quickly spread to the near East, Persia, Egypt, and northern Africa.

An Iraqi reads a magazine published in Arabic, the official language of Iraq.

Arabic consists of three different tongues: classical Arabic, colloquial Arabic, and modern standard Arabic. Classical Arabic is used in the Koran. Colloquial Arabic varies from region to region. In Iraq the colloquial tongue is called Iraqi Arabic. Each area has its own version of spoken Arabic, and people from different regions often find it difficult to understand one another when they speak in their local tongues. Modern standard Arabic is the official written form in Iraq and other Arab countries.

Arabic has an alphabet of 29 letters—26 consonants and three vowels. Arabic is written from right to left, and there is no difference between capital and small letters.

Some Arab words may not be as foreign as they sound. Due to the early Islamic conquests of various countries and to centuries of trade between the Middle East and Europe, several Western languages, such as English, French, German, Italian, Portuguese, and Spanish, have adopted some Arabic words.

Arabic words used in English include arsenal, cotton, giraffe, guitar, influenza, lime, magazine, sofa, and sugar.

BODY LANGUAGE

Nonverbal communication is an important part of interpersonal interaction in Iraq. Gestures and facial expressions may convey thoughts and feelings that are not expressed in words or may confirm the meaning of something that has been said.

Iraqis use their eyes and hands as they speak, to emphasize a point. In a conversation, Iraqis often stand closer to each other (*below*) and touch each other on the arm more often than people from many Western cultures ordinarily do. Traditionally, Iraqis also hold hands when talking to someone of the same sex, even if they are virtual strangers. Women generally do not use gestures as much as men do.

Iraqis greet people with a lot of enthusiasm. Members of the same sex kiss each other on the cheek or embrace each other. However, members of the opposite sex greet without physical contact. Even married couples traditionally avoid showing affection through gestures when they greet each other in public.

The boxes on the facing page show a few universal Arab gestures and their meanings:

1. When an Iraqi, or any Muslim for that matter, places his or her right hand over the heart after shaking hands with you, the person is expressing sincerity.

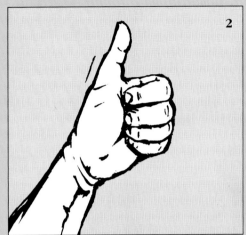

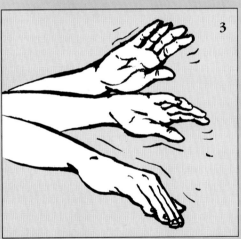

2. A raised fist with an extended thumb is a sign of victory.

3. If someone holds the right hand out, palm facing down, and moves it up and down, the person is probably telling you to be quiet.

4. If the person moves the forefinger of the right hand from right to left, he or she is saying no.

Other signs that mean a negative response include: raising the eyebrows and tilting the head back; and making clicking sounds with the tongue.

Holding the right hand out while opening and closing the palm means come here; moving the right hand, palm facing down, away from the body means go away.

A colorful spread of Arabic literature in a shop.

CONVERSATIONS

It is not common in Iraq for a man and a woman who are not close acquaintances to converse with each other. Unlike in Western cultures, men and women in Iraq rarely interact in public places such as cafés, cinemas, or restaurants.

When Iraqis converse with their friends, it is customary for them to ask each other personal questions, about the other person's marriage, children, and salary, for example. While a Westerner might find such questions intrusive even among friends, an Iraqi would be offended by the reverse—not being asked such questions.

Iraqis also tend to repeat important information when conversing or to interrupt if they have something important to say; nor would they be offended by being interrupted. When more than two close friends get together, their conversation is likely to be loud and animated.

A Kurdish man. Saddam Hussein's "ethnic cleansing" program forced the Kurds to give up their Kurdish names and adopt Arab names.

NAMES

Iraqi names are long; they include a first name, the father's name, the paternal grandfather's name, and the family name. People are addressed by their first name, which may be preceded by Mr., Mrs., Dr., or Miss. Parents are often politely addressed by their eldest son's name preceded by their parental title: "Umm" for the mother; "Abu" for the father. So the parents of a boy named Abdi would be called Umm Abdi and Abu Abdi.

After marriage, an Iraqi woman does not legally adopt her husband's name. Instead, she retains her mother's family name.

Names often indicate not only a person's family but their religious affiliation and country of origin as well. Iraqis with Western names are Christians, while names beginning with "Abdel" or containing "deen" belong to Muslims.

Men often have the same first and third name because they are named after their paternal grandfather. An English equivalent of this pattern might be Thomas Samuel Thomas Jones.

When an Iraqi's name becomes too long, a few parts of the person's name will be dropped. As a rule, his or her father's name and family name will be retained, but the others can be eliminated. Because of this practice, children of the same family often have different names or a different combination of names.

ARTS

IRAQ HAS AN extensive artistic history. The site of the first great civilization in the world, Iraq has produced inspiring literature, beautiful crafts and carpets, and grand architectural styles.

As archeologists continue to excavate the ruins of ancient Mesopotamian cities, more exciting historical discoveries are being made each year.

One famous Mesopotamian work of art is the Ishtar Gate, one of eight built by Nebuchadnezzar II. The gate is covered with blue glazed bricks and reliefs of bulls, dragons, and lions dedicated to Babylon's deities. The artwork on the gate was produced in fine detail. A reconstruction of the Ishtar Gate resides in the Pergamon Museum in Berlin, Germany.

ISLAMIC ART

Islamic art forbids the artist to portray any human or animal forms. That is why Islamic art depicts repeated patterns such as flowers or geometric designs. Many pieces of Islamic art contain Koranic inscriptions, and beautiful Arabic script adorns most of the pieces.

Islamic pottery is colorful and ornate. Materials used in the production of pots range from bronze to earthenware. Gold and silver were absent in ancient Islamic art, because these materials were strictly forbidden by Prophet Muhammad.

Carpets are some of the most magnificent artifacts in Islamic art. They are woven from fine threads in magnificent colors and are the object of many stories in Iraqi culture.

Above: **An Iraqi jewelry maker. Gold jewelry was first worn by the ancient Sumerians.**

Opposite: **A man handles paintings depicting people and objects in everyday life in Iraq: camels, marshes, and Bedouins.**

The clean simple lines of Islamic architecture are often adorned with intricate designs and filled with a dazzling array of colors on handpainted tiles.

EARLY ISLAMIC ART When the Muslim conquerors overthrew the Sassanid dynasty in A.D. 637, they inherited the state treasury. To increase their prestige, they used their newfound wealth to commission many works of art and architecture.

Wealthy Mesopotamians hired artists to weave beautiful carpets of special design for the family. In the middle of the eighth century, pottery and the textile industry became popular in the Islamic art circle. More wealthy citizens and the royal family hired talented artists to create innovative and elaborate designs. Their generous patronage of the arts encouraged artists to develop new modes of artistic expression. This inspired the great variety of Islamic art that people have appreciated for centuries.

Some of the commissioned artifacts included glass goblets or bowls decorated with elaborate designs in bright colors. Islamic glasswork ranged from bottles and drinking glasses to vases to flasks and pitchers, and from painted to colored to copper- or silver-stained. Islamic glassmakers used a variety of techniques that included gilding and enamelling.

As a patron's art collection grew, he often commissioned the construction of a museum to house the valuable artifacts. The citizens of the community were invited to these museums to view the artworks on display. Generous patrons gave their private museums to their cities or to Muslim institutions, for the benefit of the entire community.

VISUAL ARTS

Television, film, painting, and sculpture are the main visual arts of modern Iraq. The popularity of television and film in Iraqi culture has greatly increased in recent years. After the war in 2003, a U.S. media operation replaced an Iraqi television channel, providing local and world news via satellite. This new channel reported directly to the U.S. military.

Painting and sculpture are traditional Iraqi arts. Most paintings are housed in museums or homes in cities around the country. Under the Baathist regime, paintings and statues of Saddam Hussein appeared all over the nation.

When Baghdad fell to U.S. forces in April 2003, some Iraqis celebrated the end of Hussein's regime by pulling down his statue. Others defaced images of him on murals and posters elsewhere in the city. Looters took advantage of the chaos to raid Iraq's national museum, and priceless pieces such as sacred bowls, scrolls, statues, and vases were either damaged or lost.

Islamic art transformed Arabic calligraphy into an art form. Wall decorations containing Koranic verses hang in the homes of many Muslims.

95

MUSIC

Traditional instruments used to make Iraqi music include the drums, fiddle, lute, oud, and violin. During Baghdad's days of glory, its music influenced Arab-Islamic performance styles that spread as far as Spain. There are modern Iraqi musicians who have gained fame in the Arab world. They have to work abroad, because there is limited access to modern technology in Iraq due to wars and sanctions. Despite such restrictions, Iraq boasts a national symphony, opera house, and theaters that are packed during performances. Plays often depict the trauma and humor experienced by Iraqis in their daily struggles.

Some Iraqi percussion instruments.

LITERATURE

Early Iraqi literature originated as stories passed down from one generation to the next. These stories have contributed to Middle Eastern and Western literature throughout history. Stories, places, and books in the Bible, such as the Garden of Eden, the Psalms, and the Song of Solomon, have strong connections to Mesopotamian culture. Many Greek epic poems and myths, such as *The Iliad* and *Aesop's Fables,* are also based on Mesopotamian stories.

Iraq's most famous pieces of literature are the *Epic of Gilgamesh* and *A Thousand and One Nights.* The first is an Akkadian epic poem that tells of the adventures of Gilgamesh, the ruler of Erech, who tried to attain immortality. *A Thousand and One Nights* is a collection of thrilling stories of voyages, romance, and adventure. While a lot of Iraq's oral literature has been recorded and reproduced, Iraqis still enjoy literature through the art of storytelling.

Iraqi literature experienced a rebirth in the 1950s when, after centuries of cultural decay following the end of the Abbasid caliphate, many brilliant works were written. Besides the great increase in volume, the literature reflected a changing style. Epic stories were replaced by short stories that were filled with the everyday struggles and experiences of people in Iraq. Iraqi poetry styles also developed into the nonrhyming personalized form that was already popular in the Western world.

A fountain sculpture re-creates an episode from *Ali Baba and the Forty Thieves.*

CRAFTS

Handicrafts are a popular art form in Iraq. The main handicrafts made by Iraqis are blankets, jewelry, leather, pottery, and rugs.

In villages and small towns, women make handicrafts as a leisure and social activity. They gather with their children in the afternoon to make household items, such as colorful hand-woven rugs and blankets. Several households often share ownership of a pottery wheel that is used to make bowls, jugs, and ornamental objects.

Handicrafts with nature motifs. Iraqi folk artists display their works at annual art fairs.

ARCHEOLOGICAL DIGS

Iraq is an archeologist's treasure trove. The discovery of Mesopotamian ruins has allowed archeologists, historians, and the people of Iraq to better understand the complex and rich culture of Mesopotamia. Less than 10 percent of Iraq's 25,000 historical sites have been excavated, which means great potential for further discovery and revelation.

NIPPUR In 1990 archeologists uncovered a temple in the ancient city of Nippur. The temple was dedicated to Gula, the Babylonian goddess of healing. This suggested that the temple must have been a hospital or healing center. Within the temple, archeologists discovered ancient artifacts such as a bronze dog figurine with an inscription to Gula, and statues of people holding their stomach, throat, or back as if in physical pain. Archeologists believe that the inhabitants of Nippur and the nearby cities came to the temple for medical treatment. Tablets and statues with

inscriptions allow historians to study the ancient practice of medicine, the use of herbs and plants, and the roles of doctors and magicians.

MASHKAN-SHAPIR In early 1989 archeologists discovered the ruins of Mashkan-Shapir between the Tigris and Euphrates rivers. Historians believe that Mashkan-Shapir was a major Mesopotamian city around 2000 B.C. It was destroyed around 1720 B.C.

Mashkan-Shapir was surrounded by a thick wall with hidden gates. Clay tablets and cylinders bearing Sumerian cuneiform were left along the wall. Many of the tablets were dedicated to Nergal, the ancient Babylonian god of death.

Within the city walls, the remains of a cemetery, palace, and temple were found. The discovery of employees' recorded hours on the city's walls and clay tablets tells about the work ethic and lifestyle of the Mesopotamians. Elaborate canals, streets, and neighborhoods suggest that Mashkan-Shapir had an advanced government.

CENSORSHIP OF THE ARTS

After it seized power in 1968, the Baathist regime introduced the citizens of Iraq to several previously unknown luxuries, including modern healthcare, advanced technology, and improved education. Art museums, such as the Saddam Hussein Art Center (*above*), were founded in Baghdad and other cities, and an institute of fine arts, a music and ballet school, and a national symphony orchestra were built in Baghdad.

The Baathist regime exercised strict control over the arts. There was government censorship of books, films, and newspapers. Foreign journalists reporting in Iraq were closely watched by government officials. Broadcasts by such journalists were liable to be censored, especially if their reports were on sensitive matters. Iraqi journalists could expect severe reprisals for commenting on any matter remotely deemed as being anti-government. The constitutional right of free speech was a mere fallacy.

Literature and films had been equally censored under the Baathists. Artists were careful to avoid any negative reflections on the government or Saddam Hussein. This curtailed the publication efforts of many citizens. Some authors in Iraq preferred to sacrifice artistic integrity rather than risk punishment by the Iraqi government.

With the end of the Baathist regime in 2003, for the first time in more than 30 years, the Iraqi people could begin to hope for a new era of artistic discovery

ARCHITECTURE

Architectural styles in Iraq vary from modern to quaint and majestic to plain. Many high-rise apartment complexes and business offices have been built in Baghdad. In contrast, Iraqi villages and small towns have simple, low buildings.

The architectural design of Iraqi Islamic shrines and their landscapes is amazingly beautiful. The shrine is covered with detailed mosaics in bright colors, and its high, arched entrance is supported by tall, strong pillars. Above the entrance are hundreds of mirrors arranged to reflect the sunlight. Around the shrine is a courtyard enclosed by a wall that is topped with exquisitely carved golden domes and minarets. Two of the most famous shrines in Iraq are at Karbala and Najaf.

An old building in Iraq with shuttered windows and screens for privacy and ventilation.

101

LEISURE

IRAQIS ENJOY A VARIETY of leisure activities, depending on which part of the country they live in. People in the northern region take advantage of the steep mountains and cooler climate for outdoor leisure activities such as hiking and camping. People in the more watery regions around the Tigris and Euphrates rivers take to fishing and swimming in summer. People in the cities visit museums, bazaars, and shopping malls.

However, one leisure pursuit unites all of Iraq's regions—the national favorite sport of soccer.

Left: **A crowded teahouse in Mosul, northern Iraq.**

Opposite: **Iraqis socialize at the Kadhimain Shrine.**

COMPANIONSHIP

Visiting friends and relatives is a popular leisure activity for Iraqis; most people set aside time every day or once a week for visits. Children and teenagers spend time together playing sports and games and watching television. Young adults catch up with friends and relatives at elegant restaurants and dancing establishments. Older Iraqis spend time talking with their peers. Regardless of the activity Iraqis choose, they place great importance in spending their free time with those they care about.

STORYTELLING

Iraqis love to tell stories. They tell tales of fortune, luck, sorrow, and religious significance. The most popular story in Iraq is *A Thousand and One Nights,* which was first told in Mesopotamia during the reign of Caliph Harun al-Rashid.

The story begins with a king, Shahryar, who develops a distrust and hatred for all women after he is shocked by his wife's infidelity. From then on, Shahryar marries a new woman every day and has her killed the next morning. He continues to do this for years, until Scheherazade, the daughter of his minister, offers to marry him in an attempt to stop the daily killing of innocent women.

On their first night together, before Shahryar goes to sleep, Scheherazade tells him an exciting story. But she stops just before the climax. Shahryar becomes so anxious to find out how the story ends that he does not

Sindbad was a legendary explorer who had thrilling adventures in his journeys around the world.

SINDBAD THE SAILOR'S SEVEN JOURNEYS

Stories from *A Thousand and One Nights* have been translated into many languages and made into films. One of the most popular characters from the collection is Sindbad the Sailor, who makes seven journeys across land and sea, overcoming danger and disaster with wit and strength.

Sindbad first leaves Baghdad in search of adventure and wealth. His ship lands on a beautiful island that resembles Paradise but turns out to be a sleeping fish. When the fish wakes up, all of the men except Sindbad escape on the ship. His crew presumes him dead, and Sindbad lives on an island with a king, until he is able to return to his home.

On his second journey, Sindbad is deserted on an island with giant birds, poisonous serpents, and magnificent diamonds. He escapes the perilous island with several large diamonds and becomes a wealthy man with the sale of the gems.

On his third journey, Sindbad encounters vicious apes, an angry giant, an ogre, and a deadly serpent. Once again, he escapes unharmed, finds precious goods, and returns to Baghdad even more wealthy.

Sindbad's fourth journey brings him to the island of the Magis and their king. Visitors to this mysterious island are fed excessive amounts of food until they become very fat. When the men reach a certain weight, the king roasts and eats them. Sindbad leaves the island and finds jewels on another island before returning home.

On his fifth journey, Sindbad discovers an island of gigantic pumpkins and citizens who pelt apes with pebbles. After spending time in this strange land, Sindbad takes some coconuts and returns to Baghdad.

During his sixth journey, Sindbad once again becomes a shipwreck victim. He lands on a beautiful island with lakes and mountains. The island, Sarandib, is ruled by a generous king who gives Sindbad a position of honor. But Sindbad eventually misses his homeland and returns to Baghdad.

Sindbad's final journey takes him back to Sarandib bearing gifts for the king. On the passage home, his ship is captured by demons and Sindbad is sold as a slave. Sindbad the slave discovers a valley of elephant tusks, sells the tusks for his freedom, and returns to Baghdad to stay, never travelling in search of adventure again.

kill Scheherazade. Every night, for many nights, Scheherazade tells the king a bedtime story but withholds the ending until the next morning. Eventually, the king grows to love her and does not have her killed. Her exciting tales of adventure, love, fortune, princes, kings, and queens are the stories that have come to be known as *A Thousand and One Nights*, or *The Arabian Nights' Entertainment*. One of Scheherazade's most well-known stories tells about the famous adventurer Sindbad.

SPORTS

Iraqi participation in sports has grown in recent decades, but political turmoil has made it difficult for many athletes to excel internationally. Iraqis' favorite sport is soccer, known to most of the world as football. There is also a growing interest in basketball, boating, boxing, and volleyball.

SOCCER The most popular sport in the world is also the favorite sport of the Iraqis. In 1986 Iraq qualified for the soccer world cup competition, which was held in Mexico. Iraq became the first country in soccer history to qualify by playing all its competitive games in venues outside Iraq due to the Iraq-Iran War.

Iraq is a member of the Asian Football Confederation, which was founded in 1954. Iraq also takes part in the confederation's Asian Cup competition, which is staged every four years.

Soccer has been a welcome distraction in the turmoil of sanctions and wars in the last two decades. Soon after the war in 2003, Iraq's national team was reassembled and began training for the 2004 Olympics. Due to a lack of infrastructure in Iraq, the players trained in Dubai in the United Arab Emirates. Iraq's professional soccer players continue to perform, with the support of thousands of boisterous fans at matches between local clubs as well as at international games.

OTHER SPORTS Iraqis enjoy swimming and boating at Iraq's two major rivers and in the Persian Gulf. The warmer temperatures in the southern regions allow Iraqis to enjoy water sports for most of the year. However, the destruction caused by the Iraq-Iran War and the gulf wars has curtailed many water-related leisure activities in southern Iraq.

BAZAARS AND MUSEUMS

Baghdad is famous for its bazaars. Although most cities and villages in the country have them, Baghdad's are the largest and have the widest selection.

Visiting a bazaar, one is surrounded by throngs of people searching for the best deal. The bazaars offer a sumptuous array of fruit, fresh meat, and exotic spices. They attract Iraqis from all socioeconomic groups, although the wealthy families usually send someone to shop for them. The prices of items at the bazaars are usually arrived at through a heated bargaining process between the buyer and the seller.

Browsing of a different kind takes place in the museums. As the cradle of civilization, Iraq is the custodian of ancient artifacts that record human history from as early as 12,000 B.C.

Iraq's museums house some of the finest antique pieces of art, which include articles found at archeological digs. Exquisite jewels, elaborate thrones, and fancy combs from the many caliphs, kings, and rulers of Iraq are displayed. Many of these ancient artifacts were damaged during the war in 2003, and many more were stolen by looters in the chaos after the war. The loss of these artifacts represented a permanent and immense cultural loss.

RURAL ACTIVITIES

Unlike the city dwellers of Iraq, residents of the small villages and towns scattered around the country live a relatively simple life steeped in tradition. Men and women in the rural areas generally keep to their own gender in their daily occupations, including their leisure activities.

ACTIVITIES FOR MEN Most rural towns are located along one of the twin rivers, where fish are abundant. Men spend a lot of time hunting and fishing with friends. This is not just a good way to socialize; it is also possible to provide the family with food from the day's hunt or fishing. Hunting and fishing trips are exciting, and young boys eagerly await the day when their father will take them on such an expedition.

The men are usually responsible for buying food at the markets and bazaars. On market days, groups of men spend the day together while leisurely shopping for food.

ACTIVITIES FOR WOMEN Women in small villages and towns visit one another almost every day. While their husbands are away from home, working or relaxing with other men, the women gather to talk, cook, or make handicrafts.

The women also take care of and plan activities for those among their children who are not yet in school.

Above: **Marsh Arab children amuse themselves playing on boats.**

Opposite: **Baghdad's carpets are well-known, and a wide array can be found at its bazaars.**

FESTIVALS

FESTIVALS IN IRAQ are traditionally joyous occasions with family and friends gathered for feasting and merrymaking. However, the scale of celebration has diminished since 1990 due to trade sanctions, with most of Iraq's population surviving on earnings too meager to hold lavish parties.

Many festivals in Iraq celebrate secular events such as the nation's independence, but most have a religious significance. The dates of the Islamic festivals are determined by the Islamic lunar calendar rather than by the Gregorian calendar. Therefore, these special days may coincide with different Gregorian dates.

Friday is a holy day for Muslims. Most business offices and all government institutions close every Friday. The only businesses that remain open are those managed by non-Muslims.

Opposite: **Iraqi children celebrate Eid al-Fitr at an amusement park in Baghdad.**

FESTIVALS AND HOLIDAYS IN IRAQ

The dates of the Islamic festivals are stated according to the Islamic calendar, which like the Gregorian calendar has 12 months. But the same festivals fall on different Gregorian dates, because the Islamic month, and thus the Islamic year, is slightly shorter.

ISLAMIC FESTIVALS

1 Muharram	The Tree at the Boundary
10 Muharram	Ashura
12 Rabiul Awal	Maulid an-Nabi (Prophet Muhammad's birthday)
Ramadan	Ramadan fast
1 Syawal	Eid al-Fitr
10 Zulhijjah	Eid al-Adha

NATIONAL HOLIDAYS

January 1	New Year's Day
January 6	Army Day
July 17	Anniversary of the Revolution
October 3	Independence from British mandate

CHRISTIAN FESTIVALS

April	Easter (exact date varies)
December 25	Christmas

Shi'a Muslim pilgrims embrace the shrine of Hussein.

MUHARRAM

The Islamic New Year is celebrated in the month of Muharram, the first month of the Islamic calendar year. Muharram is especially important to Shi'a Muslims.

OH, HUSSEIN! OH, HUSSEIN! During Muharram, Shi'a Muslims visit the shrine of Hussein to honor the grandson of Prophet Muhammad. Shi'a Muslims believe that Hussein was killed in battle for his religion. Hussein's story is recounted on the first nine nights of Muharram. As believers listen to the highly emotional story, many cry and shout, "Oh, Hussein! Oh, Hussein!"

Other events commemorate Hussein's death. The people reenact his daughter's marriage and his burial. One of the most intriguing events of Muharram is a street procession of Shi'a Muslim men beating themselves and one another with chains, belts, and sticks. They willingly undergo such physical pain to imitate the sufferings of Hussein.

THE TREE AT THE BOUNDARY During the first week of Muharram, Shi'a Muslims tell the story of the Tree at the Boundary. According to legend, on the first night of Muharram, an angel shakes a tree at the boundary of Paradise and Earth. Each leaf on the tree represents a living person. If a leaf falls while the angel shakes the tree, the person whose name appears on the leaf will die in the coming year.

No one knows which leaves fall off the tree. But when someone dies, Shi'a Muslims believe that that person's name was inscribed on a leaf that fell off the Tree at the Boundary on the first evening of Muharram.

ASHURA The tenth day of Muharram is called Ashura. After the ceremonial reenactment of Hussein's death, Iraqi Muslim women begin preparations for a feast for the men and children.

The whole village or family gathers at nightfall for a big feast. The day is also associated with the landing of Noah's Ark. The mourning surrounding the death of Hussein is replaced by festivities to celebrate the perpetuation of humankind.

The Muslims, like the Christians and the Jews, believe that Noah gathered two of every living creature in the world and built an ark to protect them from the great flood. When the flood came, it destroyed all the creatures of the earth except those inside the ark. Noah and his crew survived inside the ark for 40 days, after which they landed on dry ground and began life anew. Iraqi Muslims celebrate the landing of Noah's Ark on Ashura.

A woman and her child receive free milk from the mosque during Ramadan under Saddam Hussein's regime.

113

The Grand Mosque of Mecca, where hundreds of thousands of Muslims converge every year to perform the hajj. Mecca was the place where Prophet Muhammad was born, where he grew up, and where the Koran was revealed to him.

RAMADAN

The fourth pillar of Islam is the observance of Ramadan, the month when Muslims fast from sunrise to sunset.

Fasting Muslims remind themselves of their dependence on God and His blessings and draw closer to Him by saying more prayers, giving more money to charity, and reading the Koran more often.

Fasting requires a lot of self-discipline, especially when there is an abundance of food. Fasting enables Muslims to develop compassion for those who do not have enough to eat.

The time to break the fast is indicated by the sound of a cannon explosion, usually broadcast on the radio, which follows the evening call to prayer announced at sunset by the muezzin at the mosque.

At the end of Ramadan, everyone gives alms, and the wealthy usually invite the less fortunate into their homes to feast with them.

EID AL-FITR

Eid al-Fitr (eed ahl-FITTER) is one of the biggest holidays in the Islamic calendar. It marks the end of the fasting month of Ramadan. Muslims celebrate the three-day Eid al-Fitr by feasting. The wealthy stay home during Eid al-Fitr and invite friends and relatives over to feast, while the less wealthy, mostly those in the rural areas, buy new clothes and dine with their richer friends.

MAULID AN-NABI

Maulid an-Nabi (MAW-lid ahn-NEH-bee) celebrates the birthday of Prophet Muhammad. On this holiday, older Muslims relate the series of events that accompanied the birth of the prophet.

Angels descended upon the earth to assist in Prophet Muhammad's delivery. He was born with a light that lit up the space between the East and the West. The light illuminated the palaces of Syria, Lebanon, Palestine, and Jordan. Gazing into his face, Prophet Muhammad's mother saw that he shone like the moon and smelled of the finest perfume.

On the night that he was born, the earth shook until the pagan idols in Mecca collapsed and the fire in a Persian temple that had been worshiped for a thousand years was extinguished.

EID AL-ADHA

Eid al-Adha (eed ahl-AHD-ha) occurs in Zulhijjah, the 12th month of the Islamic year, when Muslims visit Mecca, in Saudi Arabia, for the hajj. Every year on Eid al-Adha, Muslims celebrate the patriarch Abraham's love for God by visiting the graves of their relatives and giving food to the poor.

The story of Abraham's faith goes like this: To test Abraham's loyalty, God told him to sacrifice his son Ishmael. Abraham told Ishmael about this command, and Ishmael asked his father to do it. As Abraham tearfully raised his knife, a miracle happened, and in Ishmael's place was a sheep instead. Abraham proved his faith in God, and God spared Ishmael.

A goat or sheep is sacrificed on Eid al-Adha to commemorate Abraham's love for God. The meat is then distributed to the poor.

FAMILY CELEBRATIONS

WEDDINGS The most exciting nonreligious celebration in Iraq is the wedding. Wedding festivities start a few days before the marriage ceremony, as relatives, friends, and acquaintances host parties to honor the couple.

On the day of the wedding, the bride and groom marry in a small ceremony, with only their relatives and closest friends present. After the ceremony, the wedding party parades through the streets, with residents cheering them to the newlyweds' home, where the bride and groom consummate their marriage.

The party continues to celebrate while waiting for the young couple. When the newlyweds emerge from their home, the party proceeds to a reception, and the celebration often lasts until the early morning hours.

BIRTHS Three days after the birth of a baby, friends and family visit the parents and the baby, usually bringing gifts for the child.

The birth of a boy in Iraq is celebrated more than the birth of a girl. With the birth of each male child, superstitious rites are performed to provide protection throughout the boy's life. Foreign visitors and women without children are discouraged from attending the birth festivities, as this is considered bad luck.

AL' KHATMA The religious festival that Iraqi Muslims take most pride in is a child's reading of the Koran. Children diligently study the Koran for a year or more in preparation for al' Khatma, so that they can read the Koran without making any mistakes.

The reading of the Koran is a very difficult task. Children go through many sessions, boys reading to men and girls to women, until they complete the entire holy book. This requires a great deal of discipline and dedication, and the child's success is seen as a major accomplishment. Muslims believe that the reading of the Koran is the first step in receiving God's blessings and that the true sign of a gift from God is a person's ability to fully understand the meaning of Islam's holy book.

The al' Khatma ceremony is a very solemn occasion. The child receives the undivided attention of his or her peers and elders while reading. When a boy has read the Koran without error, he earns the title *hafiz* (HAH-fizz), while a girl who reads the Koran perfectly is called *hafizah* (HAH-fi-ZAH).

After the child has successfully read the Koran, the ceremony becomes a festival in his or her honor. The men usually hold a lunch for the boy, while the women celebrate with an afternoon tea for the girl. Friends and relatives of the *hafiz* or *hafizah* attend the festival and shower gifts and money on the honorary guest. All the attendants dress in colorful clothes and spend the afternoon celebrating the child's accomplishment.

The Koran is reverently placed on a stand and usually read sitting down.

FOOD

THE STAPLES IN the Iraqi diet are wheat, barley, and rice. Women in small villages use wheat to make bread; barley is a main ingredient in many Iraqi dishes; and rice may be eaten as a main or side dish.

MEAT

The most important livestock in Iraq are sheep and goats, raised by nomadic and seminomadic groups for meat, milk, wool, and skins.

In small villages, butchers slaughter a sheep or goat every day. Villagers hurry to the butchers to claim choice cuts for their dinner. Those who go to the butchers later in the day will find only the remains of a carcass.

Iraqis cook almost every part of a sheep or goat. Delicacies include the kidneys, liver, and brain. The meat is usually cut into small strips and cooked with onions and garlic for flavor. Iraqis also enjoy mincing the meat for a stew that is served with rice. Other meats enjoyed in Iraq are fish, beef, chicken, and camel.

Since 1990 most Iraqis have survived on monthly rations of chicken, flour, sugar, and yeast. This has had a harmful effect on the health of the average Iraqi, particularly children aged 1 to 5, as their daily diet lacks many essential vitamins and nutrients. In fact, one in five Iraqi children does not live to age 5.

Islam forbids the consumption of pork, but Christians in Iraq have access to pork from Christian butchers.

Above: **Besides being beasts of burden, camels provide milk and meat for a variety of Middle Eastern foods.**

Opposite: **Street vendors wipe fruit displayed on a cart at the entrance of a bazaar in Baghdad.**

An itinerant fruit vendor sells bananas.

IRAQI KITCHENS

Kitchens in Iraq range from modern ones with microwave ovens to primitive rooms without running water or electricity. The location of a house indicates whether a kitchen is likely to be modern.

Kitchens in village homes are simple, with no running water for cooking. People collect water from the river and heat it to kill the bacteria before drinking it or using it to prepare food.

When bombing during the wars cut electricity and running water to many towns, Iraqis in those towns had to return to primitive ways of acquiring a water supply, such as collecting water from a well or river and leaving the water in the sun for a few days to minimize contamination. But many still died from drinking impure water.

Wealthy residents in the cities usually hire a cook, while the family supervises the food preparation. Upper-class Iraqi kitchens are very modern, with every electrical appliance available. The cook goes to the market to buy fresh ingredients, and meals are eaten in a dining room that is separate from the kitchen.

MEALS DURING THE FASTING MONTH

During Ramadan, Muslims have their main meals before dawn and at sunset. Before dawn, Iraqis have a simple meal of fried egg or omelette with onions, and radish and broad beans. The meal is completed with dates and other fruit, a large glass of juice, and plenty of water.

Iraqis break fast with a light meal of dates, a yogurt drink or a thick apricot juice, and a bowl of soup. They have the second main meal half an hour later. This includes a lamb, beef, or chicken stew with rice, a vegetable dish, grilled or ovenbaked fish, a salad, and bread.

After 1990 sanctions reduced Iraqi meals to meager proportions. To most Iraqis, the fasting month has made little difference in the amount of food consumed, since many of them go about their daily lives all year without much to eat.

Meat from lamb and sheep is traditionally used to prepare special dishes during feasts and festivals.

FEASTING

Iraqis express their joy in and gratitude to God by holding feasts. Two important feasts take place during the Islamic year. One commemorates the end of Ramadan; the other celebrates the pilgrimage to Mecca.

A feast to an Iraqi is a celebration equivalent to a party. No one is left out of the celebration—neighbors, relatives, and friends are invited to partake in the festivities.

Iraqi families spend hours preparing the food for the feast, and there is usually singing, dancing, and storytelling to go with the eating.

A single pita bread can be shared by a whole family. This flat, unleavened bread is cooked on a griddle.

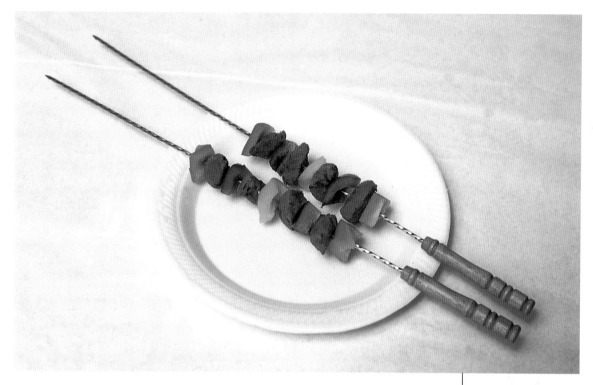

FAVORITE FOODS

A true Iraqi meal lives up to the word feast. There may be several appetizers, soups, salads, main courses, and desserts—with so many choices, an Iraqi meal often resembles a buffet.

A favorite Iraqi feast commences with salad and soup served with bread. Iraqi bread, *khubiz* (khoo-biz), is traditionally baked in a clay furnace and can make a filling meal when served with appetizers. Iraqi soups range from a thick lentil soup to a creamy chicken soup. Popular Iraqi salads include a mixture of pickled vegetables and a mixture of mashed potatoes with crushed wheat.

The main courses are simple but delicious and are often served with a tomato-based sauce mixed with okra. Kebabs, marinated lamb or chicken cubes skewered over a charcoal grill, are an all-time favorite. Fish from the Tigris is barbequed on bricks to make *masgoof* (mahs-GOOF). Other preferred dishes include roasted chicken or stewed lamb with rice.

Kebabs can be made to look colorful depending on the vegetables used.

Arab coffee pots

DRINKS AND DESSERTS

The two most popular drinks among Iraqis are coffee and tea. Both are usually served either before or after a meal, rather than with food. Iraqis generally like their coffee sweet and with fresh cream or milk.

Iraqis have an unusual tradition in the preparation of coffee. They will heat and cool the coffee nine times before serving, believing that this removes impurities. This practice is common in the smaller villages and towns, while urbanites prefer their coffee fast.

One common attribute of coffee drinking in Iraq is that it is a social activity. Iraqis like to have their coffee with family and friends at cafés, restaurants, parties, or at home.

During the summer months, most people enjoy a cool, refreshing glass of water. Soft drinks have become a luxury for most Iraqis since trade sanctions were imposed.

Although Islam forbids the consumption of alcohol, Iraq produces a very potent spirit, known as arak, from dates. Before the 1991 Gulf War,

Iraq brewed its own beer and the northern regions produced wine. But the average Iraqi today cannot afford the luxury of alcohol.

Like many other Middle Easterners, the Iraqis are renowned for their desserts. Their favorites include an assortment of pastries with creamy fillings such as ground almonds or mashed dates, thin pancakes buried in layers of fruit and syrup, and a rich semolina and cinnamon pudding called *ma'mounia.*

Iraqis have a sweet tooth. Fresh or canned fruit is often served after a meal. A favorite dessert is baklava, a layered pastry stuffed with honey and nuts.

A POPULAR IRAQI DESSERT

Ma'mounia was first made in the ninth century for a caliph who wanted a sumptuous dessert worthy of a king. His cook obliged with a pudding that remains an Iraqi favorite today. Here is a recipe for four.

2 cups sugar
3 cups water
1 teaspoon lemon juice
$^1/_2$ cup sweet butter
1 cup semolina
Whipped cream
1 teaspoon ground cinnamon

Put the sugar and the water in a large saucepan, and stir constantly over low heat until the sugar dissolves. Add the lemon juice, and bring the mixture to a boil. Reduce the heat, and simmer for about 10 minutes, until the syrup thickens slightly. In another saucepan, melt the butter, then add the semolina. Stir until the semolina is lightly fried. Pour the mixture into the syrup, stirring constantly. Simmer for another 10 minutes, then cool for 20 minutes. Spoon the mixture into small bowls, and top with a glob of whipped cream and a sprinkle of cinnamon.

THE EID AL-FITR FEAST

Iraqis traditionally celebrate the end of Ramadan with a feast on Eid al-Fitr. In a village of approximately 300 people, one or two cows and five to seven grown sheep might be slaughtered. The internal organs of the animals would be prepared in a special way, and the rest of the meat roasted over a charcoal fire, cut into small pieces, and served with vegetables and rice.

The people of the village gather in one large room to share the meal. The men sit on one side of the room or move to another room altogether to have their meal apart from the women.

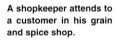

A shopkeeper attends to a customer in his grain and spice shop.

TABLE MANNERS

The Iraqis have very strict rules concerning table manners. Here are some things to do or to avoid when dining with Iraqis:

- It is offensive to use one's left hand when eating. For traditional reasons, the left hand is considered unclean.
- It is considered proper for only one person to pay the bill in a restaurant. Iraqis are embarrassed by the Western custom of splitting the bill.
- Iraqis prepare a lot of food for parties or feasts. To be polite, the guests try to eat everything in front of them.
- It is not considered rude in Iraq to eat food quickly or without utensils. In fact, it is a sign to the host or hostess that the food is delicious.
- Iraqis are extremely offended if the family pet comes near the table during the meal.
- After eating, Iraqis lavishly praise the meal and the preparation of the food.
- When attending a meal prepared by someone else, an Iraqi will invariably bring a small gift to the host as a gesture of gratitude.

SOCIAL ETIQUETTE

There are other rules that are as important as proper table manners in everyday life. The following are some general rules of Iraqi etiquette:

- Iraqis shake hands when greeting. When a man and a woman greet, the woman extends her hand first to indicate that she wants to shake hands.
- It is considered very rude to turn one's foot outward when talking to someone. Iraqis will be extremely offended if a person turns the sole of his or her foot toward them.
- If an Iraqi gives someone a gift, it should be accepted with both hands and opened in the absence of the benefactor.
- Iraqi men stand when a woman enters the room, and open doors for women. Both men and women stand when an older person enters or leaves the room.
- If someone admires an Iraqi's possession, such as a vase or small sculpture, the Iraqi will usually insist that the person take it. Therefore, it is proper etiquette to refrain from lavishly praising another's possessions.

In the cities, the wealthy may have servants prepare and serve the feast. In more modest households, it is traditionally the women who are responsible for preparing and serving the food.

Wars and sanctions have greatly toned down Eid al-Fitr festivities in Iraq. For most Iraqis, feasting is a thing of the past, until their country recovers from its wounds, under a hopefully more democratic regime.

Iraqis enjoy a pleasant lunch in the outdoors.

FOOD SHOPPING

The cities and villages of Iraq are filled with small food markets, which often form part of a larger group of markets called a bazaar, which sells a wide range of products from food to handicrafts.

The most successful food markets in Iraq sell fruit, vegetables, spices, or fresh meat. In the small villages and towns, the men do the marketing after deciding with their wives what the household needs.

Due to wars and sanctions, many Iraqis lost the means to buy food for their basic meals. They had to survive on food rations given out by Saddam Hussein's government. After the war in 2003, humanitarian aid organizations played a big part in alleviating the shortage of food that caused malnutrition and death, especially among children.

EATING OUT

One of the true pleasures in Iraqi cities is dining out in one of the fine restaurants that offer food from many countries. Iraqis also spend their afternoons sitting among friends in one of the outdoor cafés. Friends gather to sip their favorite coffee, nibble on sweets, and share news. On a hot day, the cafés provide cold lemonade and water under large umbrellas or awnings. The regular customers are often older gentlemen who spend a relaxing afternoon watching people hurry to work or shop in the bazaars.

REGIONAL FOODS

Topography and weather play a major role in determining the favorite foods of a particular region. These factors traditionally restrict Iraqis' choice of fresh foods to those that are available to them in their region. Modern transportation, however, has widened the choice.

THE TIGRIS AND EUPHRATES RIVERS The residents of the areas surrounding the two main rivers of Iraq are blessed with a daily selection of fresh fish. Another favorite in the region is milk from the *jamoosa* (jah-MOO-sah), or water buffalo. The *jamoosa's* milk is rich and is used to make yogurt and butter. The yogurt is prepared by cooling the fresh milk overnight, scraping off the top layer, and adding a yogurt starter. Within hours, the yogurt is ready for eating, cooking, or diluting with water for a delicious drink.

THE NORTHERN REGION Iraqis of the northern regions, including the Kurds, eat meat from cows or chickens. Cows receive more nourishment in the cooler north and live healthier lives. Thus, the meat and milk from these cows is delicious and rich.

The women of the northern regions prepare homemade tomato paste from homegrown tomatoes. Another regional delicacy is goat's milk, which is used to make white, preserved cheese.

CHICKEN WITH SAFFRON RICE

This recipe serves two.

1 medium onion, finely sliced
4^1/$_2$ cups water
Salt and pepper
3 to 4 chicken breasts
3 teaspoons liquid saffron
1 pinch saffron

1 teaspoon salt
6 tablespoons vegetable oil
17 ounces (480 ml) basmati long-grain rice
2 ounces (60 ml) raw, unsalted, slivered almonds
2 ounces (60 ml) raisins
1 tablespoon rose water

Put the onion, four tablespoons water, and the salt and pepper in a pan. Add the chicken. Cover and simmer over low heat for 30 minutes, until tender. Add the liquid saffron, and turn the chicken to coat. In another pan, mix the saffron, salt, 4 tablespoons oil, and remaining water. Bring to a boil over high heat. Add the rice. Return to a boil, then lower to medium heat. Cook uncovered until most of the water is absorbed. Stir from the bottom up, then cover and simmer for 15 minutes over low heat. Heat the remaining oil in another pan, and fry the almonds until slightly brown. Add the raisins, and stir for a few seconds until fluffy. Serve the chicken over the rice. Garnish with the almond-raisin mixture.

MEAT WRAPPED IN EGGPLANT

This recipe makes four servings.

2 large eggplants, washed
6 tablespoons corn oil
1 pound (approximately 450 g)
  lean ground meat
1 small onion, diced
Black pepper
1 teaspoon salt
1 medium onion, diced
1 medium tomato, peeled and
  chopped
$^1/_4$ teaspoon pepper
$^1/_2$ teaspoon turmeric
7 ounces (approximately 200
  ml) tomato sauce
$^1/_2$ cup beef or chicken stock
$^1/_4$ cup lemon juice

Preheat oven to 350°F (177°C). Cut off the ends of the eggplants, and slice each in half down the length. Heat 4 tablespoons oil in a pan. Fry the eggplant halves, then dry on paper towels on a plate. Remove some of the pulp, leaving a $^1/_2$ inch- (1 cm-) thick shell. Heat 1 tablespoon oil in a pan. Sauté the meat, small onion, black pepper, and $^1/_2$ teaspoon salt. Chop the eggplant pulp and mix with the meat. Divide the mixture into 4 portions, and fill each eggplant shell with a portion of the mixture. Put the filled shells in a baking dish. Heat 1 tablespoon oil in a pan, and sauté the medium onion. Add the chopped tomato, pepper, turmeric, and $^1/_2$ teaspoon salt. Then add the tomato sauce, stock, and lemon juice to taste. Cover, and simmer for 15 minutes. Pour the sauce over the filled shells in the baking dish. Cover with aluminum foil, and bake for 45 minutes, or until done.

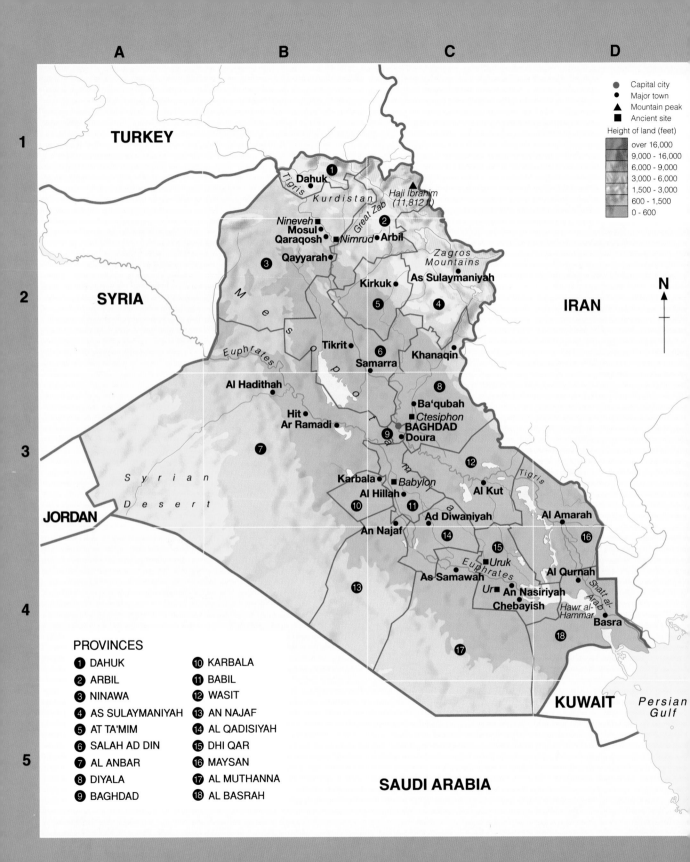

MAP OF IRAQ

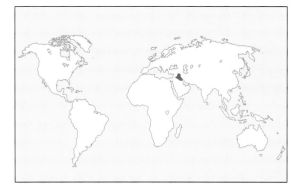

ECONOMIC IRAQ

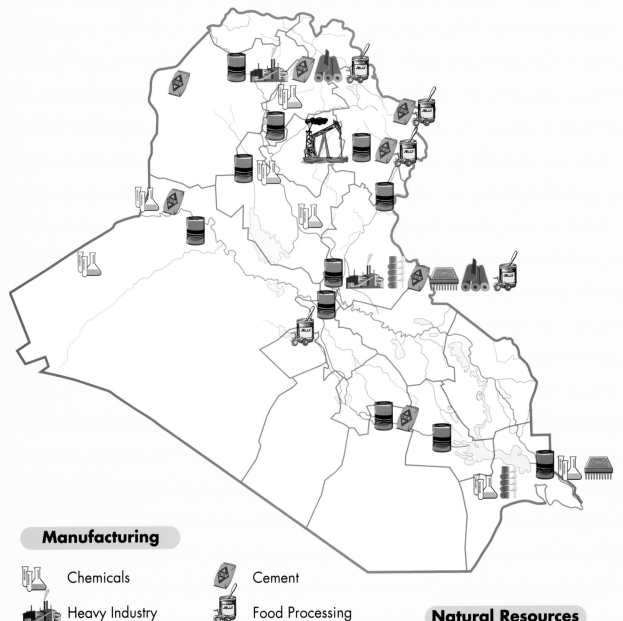

Manufacturing

 Chemicals

 Heavy Industry

 Light Industry

Petroleum Refining

 Cement

 Food Processing

Metal Processing

 Textiles

Natural Resources

 Oil and Gas

ABOUT THE ECONOMY

OVERVIEW

The Iraqi economy has depended heavily on the export of its most abundant natural resource—oil—since the early 20th century. But by the late 1900s, wars, dictatorship, and international trade sanctions had wiped out all trace of the nation's former wealth, leaving the coffers dried up like the nation's marshlands. In 2003, as Iraq sought a new government to replace Saddam Hussein's regime, the economy lay in shambles, unable to repay its war debts or feed its people.

GROSS DOMESTIC PRODUCT

$59 billion (2001)
Growth rate: -5.7 percent (2001)

AGRICULTURAL PRODUCTS

Wheat, barley, rice, vegetables, dates, cotton, cattle, sheep

INDUSTRIAL PRODUCTS

Petroleum, chemicals, textiles, food products

LABOR FORCE

6.5 million (2002)

CURRENCY

1 Iraqi dinar (IQD) = 20 dirham = 1,000 fil
Notes: ¼, ½, 1, 5, 10, 25, 50, 100, 250 dinar
Coins: 1, 5, 10, 25, 50, 100, 250 fil; ½, 1 dinar
USD 1 = IQD 0.32410 (May 2003)

INFLATION RATE

60 percent (2001)

MAIN EXPORT

Crude oil

MAIN IMPORTS

Food, medicine, manufactured goods

TRADE PARTNERS

United States, Italy, France, Spain, Australia, China, Russia

EXTERNAL DEBT

$120 billion (2002)

PORTS AND HARBORS

Basra, Khawr az Zubayr, Umm Qasr

PIPELINES

Crude oil 2,703 miles (4,350 km), natural gas 845 miles (1,360 km)

OIL PRODUCTION CAPACITY

3.5 million barrels per day (1980). The dawn of a new political era in 2003 opened the way to resuming Iraq's optimal oil output and utilizing undiscovered oil reserves. Iraq's oil production costs are among the lowest in the world.

INTERNATIONAL PARTICIPATION

International Monetary Fund (IMF), Organization of Petroleum Exporting Countries (OPEC), United Nations Educational, Scientific, and Cultural Organization (UNESCO), World Health Organization (WHO)

CULTURAL IRAQ

Great Nurid Mosque
Built in A.D. 1172, this mosque in Mosul is famed for its 170-foot (52-m) bent minaret in elaborate brickwork.

Hatra
This ancient fortified city built under the influence of the Parthian empire was also the capital of the first Arab kingdom.

Iraqi Museum
Looting after the 2003 war damaged and depleted one of the world's most important archeological collections—more than 10,000 items from Mesopotamia and other ancient civilizations—in this museum in Baghdad.

Abbasid Palace
This 13th-century palace holds the echoes of the glorious Abbassid era, when Baghdad was the center of Arab Islamic civilization.

Nineveh
This rich archeological site in Mosul was the capital of the Assyrian empire.

Arbil
This ancient city once ruled the Romans is said to be the oldest continuously inhabited city in the world.

Ctesiphon
The ruins of the capital of the Parthian and Persian empires demonstrate the splendor of Sassanian architecture.

Babylon
This great city was once ruled by Nebuchadnezzar II, who built the famous Hanging Gardens and the Ishtar Gate. This is also the site of the Tower of Babel.

Tigris River
It was here that Islam and the Assyrian and Babylonian empires rose. The Tigris—with its twin, the Euphrates—provides a livelihood to the people of Iraq, Syria, and Turkey.

Ur
Established around 2100 B. Ur was the capital of the Sumerians, one of the first known civilizations that adopted a code of conduct and law for its people.

ABOUT THE CULTURE

OFFICIAL NAME
Republic of Iraq

NATIONAL FLAG
Three equal horizontal bands of red, white, and black, with three green five-pointed stars in a horizontal line centered in the white band. The phrase *Allahu Akbar*, meaning God is great, in green Arabic script, was added during the 1991 Gulf War.

NATIONAL ANTHEM
Ardulfurataini Watan (Land of Two Rivers). Adopted in 1981. Words by Shafiq Abdul Jabar al-Kamali; music by Walid Georges Gholmieh.

CAPITAL
Baghdad

OTHER MAJOR CITIES
Basra, Mosul, Kirkuk

POPULATION
24,001,816 (2002)

LIFE EXPECTANCY
Total population 68.4 years; men 66.3 years, women 68.5 years (2002)

ETHNIC GROUPS
Arab 76 percent; Kurdish 19 percent; Turkoman 3 percent; Persian 1 percent; Assyrian or other 1 percent

RELIGIOUS GROUPS
Shi'a Muslim 53 percent; Sunni Muslim 42 percent; Christian or other 5 percent

LANGUAGES
Arabic (official); Armenian, Kurdish, Persian, Turkish (minority)

LITERACY RATE
58 percent

ISLAMIC HOLIDAYS
The Tree at the Boundary (Muharram 1), Ashura (Muharram 10), Maulid an-Nabi (Rabiul Awal 12), Eid al-Fitr (Syawal 1), Eid al-Adha (Zulhijjah 10)

NATIONAL HOLIDAYS
New Year's Day (January 1), Army Day (January 6), Anniversary of the Revolution (July 17), Independence from British mandate (October 3)

LEADERS IN POLITICS
Faisal II—last king of Iraq (1948–58)
Abdul Karim Kassem—led the revolt against the monarchy; prime minister of Iraq (1958–63)
Abd as-Salaam Arif—overthrew the first Baathist government; president of Iraq (1963–66)
Ahmad Hassan al-Bakr—first Baathist president of Iraq (1968–79)
Saddam Hussein—president and prime minister of Iraq (1979–2003)

137

TIME LINE

IN IRAQ	IN THE WORLD

IN IRAQ

9000 B.C.
Settlers cultivate wild wheat and barley, domesticate dogs and sheep.

3500 B.C.
Sumerians start the world's first known civilization, on the banks of the Euphrates.

1900 B.C.
Babylonians conquer Mesopotamia.
605 B.C.
Nebuchadnezzar II builds the Hanging Gardens and the Ishtar Gate.
331 B.C.
Alexander the Great conquers Mesopotamia.

A.D. 637
Muslims invade Mesopotamia and convert its people to Islam.
1258
Mongols attack; Islamic caliphate ends.

1534
Turks seize Mesopotamia and annex it to the Ottoman Empire.

1840
First archeological excavation

IN THE WORLD

753 B.C.
Rome is founded.

116–17 B.C.
The Roman empire reaches its greatest extent, under Emperor Trajan (98–117).

A.D. 600
Height of Mayan civilization
1000
The Chinese perfect gunpowder and begin to use it in warfare.

1530
Beginning of trans-Atlantic slave trade organized by the Portuguese in Africa
1558–1603
Reign of Elizabeth I of England
1620
Pilgrims sail the *Mayflower* to America.

1776
U.S. Declaration of Independence
1789–99
French Revolution

IN IRAQ	IN THE WORLD
	1861 U.S. Civil War begins.
	1869 The Suez Canal is opened.
	1914 World War I begins.
1917 British capture Baghdad from the Turks.	
1932 Iraq becomes an independent state.	
	1939 World War II begins.
	1945 The United States drops atomic bombs on Hiroshima and Nagasaki.
	1949 North Atlantic Treaty Organization (NATO) is formed.
	1957 Russians launch Sputnik.
1958 General Abdul Karim Kassem leads a revolution that ends the monarchy.	
	1966–69 Chinese Cultural Revolution
1968 The Baath Party takes over the government.	
1979 Saddam Hussein becomes president.	
1980 Iraq-Iran war begins.	
	1986 Nuclear power disaster at Chernobyl in Ukraine
1990 Iraq invades Kuwait.	
1991 Gulf War drives Iraqi forces out of Kuwait.	**1991** Break-up of the Soviet Union
1995 United Nations allows Iraq to export oil to buy food and medicine.	
	1997 Hong Kong is returned to China.
	2001 Terrorists crash planes in New York, Washington, D.C., and Pennsylvania.
2003 U.S.-led strike ousts Saddam Hussein.	

GLOSSARY

abaaya (ah-BAH-yah)
A long dark-colored cloak worn by women that covers them from head to ankle.

cuneiform
The oldest known writing system in the world, used extensively in Mesopotamia and Persia. The characters have a wedge-shaped appearance.

Eid al-Adha (eed ahl-AHD-ha)
The Islamic festival celebrated in remembrance of Abraham's near-sacrifice of his son Ishmael and God's sparing of Ishmael's life in recognition of Abraham's faith.

Eid al-Fitr (eed ahl-FITTER)
The Islamic festival celebrated to end the month-long fast of Ramadan.

hajj
The pilgrimage to Mecca, required of all Muslims who are able to go.

Ka'bah (kah-AH-bah)
The holiest Islamic shrine in the world, situated in Mecca, Saudi Arabia.

Koran
The holy book of Islam. Muslims believe that it was dictated by God to Prophet Muhammad.

Mesopotamia
Ancient Iraq; the region between the two main rivers of Iraq, the Tigris and the Euphrates.

muezzin
A man who calls Muslims to prayer from a mosque, via loudspeakers.

Muharram (MOO-hah-rahm)
The Islamic New Year and the first month of the Islamic calendar.

Ramadan (rah-mah-DHAN)
The ninth month of the Islamic calendar, a time of fasting and atonement for sins.

sheikh
The leader of a village or tribe.

Shi'a
The majority Islamic sect in Iraq that recognizes Prophet Muhammad's son-in-law, Ali, as his heir.

Sunni
The minority Islamic sect in Iraq that recognizes another of Prophet Muhammad's relatives as his heir.

surah
A chapter in the Koran.

thobe (THOH-bay)
A long, loose, plain caftan with long sleeves that is traditionally worn by men.

ziggurat (ZIG-goo-raht)
An ancient Mesopotamian temple tower shaped like a pyramid with many storeys.

FURTHER INFORMATION

BOOKS

Al-Takarli, Fuad. *The Long Way Back*. New York: AUC Press, 2001.

Chaliand, Gerard. *A People Without a Country: The Kurds and Kurdistan*. Massachusetts: Interlink Publishing, 1993.

Dabrowska, Karen. *Iraq: The Bradt Travel Guide*. Bucks, UK: Bradt Travel Guides, 2002.

Haidar, Mahdi. *The World of Saddam Hussein*. Cologne: Al-Kamel Verlag, 2003.

Hiro, Philip. *The Longest War: The Iran-Iraq Military Conflict*. New York: Routledge, 1991.

Mikhail, Mona N. *Images of Arab Women: Fact and Fiction*. Washington, D.C.: Three Continents Press, Inc., 1990.

Nakash, Yitzhak. *Shi'is of Iraq*. New Jersey: Princeton University Press, 2003.

Pitt, William Rivers and Scott Ritter. *War on Iraq: What Team Bush Doesn't Want You to Know*. Manhattan: Context Books, 2002.

WEBSITES

AlterNet: War on Iraq (alternative views). www.alternet.org/waroniraq

Arab.Net (click on the Iraqi flag). www.arab.net/index.html

Central Intelligence Agency World Factbook (select Iraq from the country list). www.cia.gov/cia/publications/factbook

Children of Iraq: A Newsletter about the Plight of the Children. www.childrenofiraq.org

Electronic Iraq (from Voices in the Wilderness and Electronic Intifada). http://electroniciraq.net/news

Iraq Daily (newspaper). www.iraqdaily.com

Iraq Watch (news on Iraq's development of weapons of mass destruction). www.iraqwatch.org

Library of Congress: Federal Research Division: Country Studies (select Iraq from the country list). http://memory.loc.gov/frd/cs/cshome.html

University of Chicago: Oriental Institute: Archeological Site Photography: Mesopotamia. www-oi.uchicago.edu/OI/IS/SANDERS/PHOTOS/meso_map.html

U.S. Congressional Research Service reports on Iraq and Saddam Hussein. www.iraqresearch.com/html/reports.html

U.S. Department of State International Information Programs: Iraq. http://usinfo.state.gov/regional/nea/iraq

VIDEOS

From Mesopotamia to Iraq. Seattle: Arab Film Distribution, 1991.

Marooned in Iraq. New York: Wellspring Media, Inc., 2003.

BIBLIOGRAPHY

Bratman, Fred. *War in the Persian Gulf.* Brookfield: Millbrook Press, 1991.

Childs, N. *The Gulf War.* Vero Beach: Rourke, 1991.

Foster, Leila M. *Iraq.* Chicago: Childrens Press, 1990.

Salzman, Marian and Ann O'Reilly. *War and Peace in the Persian Gulf: What Teenagers Want to Know.* Princeton: Peterson's Guides, 1991.

Tripp, Charles. *A History of Iraq.* Cambridge: University Press, 2000.

Iraq in Pictures. Visual Geography Series. Minneapolis: Lerner Publications Company, 1990.

INDEX